NORTHAW

... AND SO MUCH MORE

First published by LWCS Publications 2010

ISBN 978-0-9567631-0-5

Typeset by Marque Design Limited

Printed by Good News Digital Books

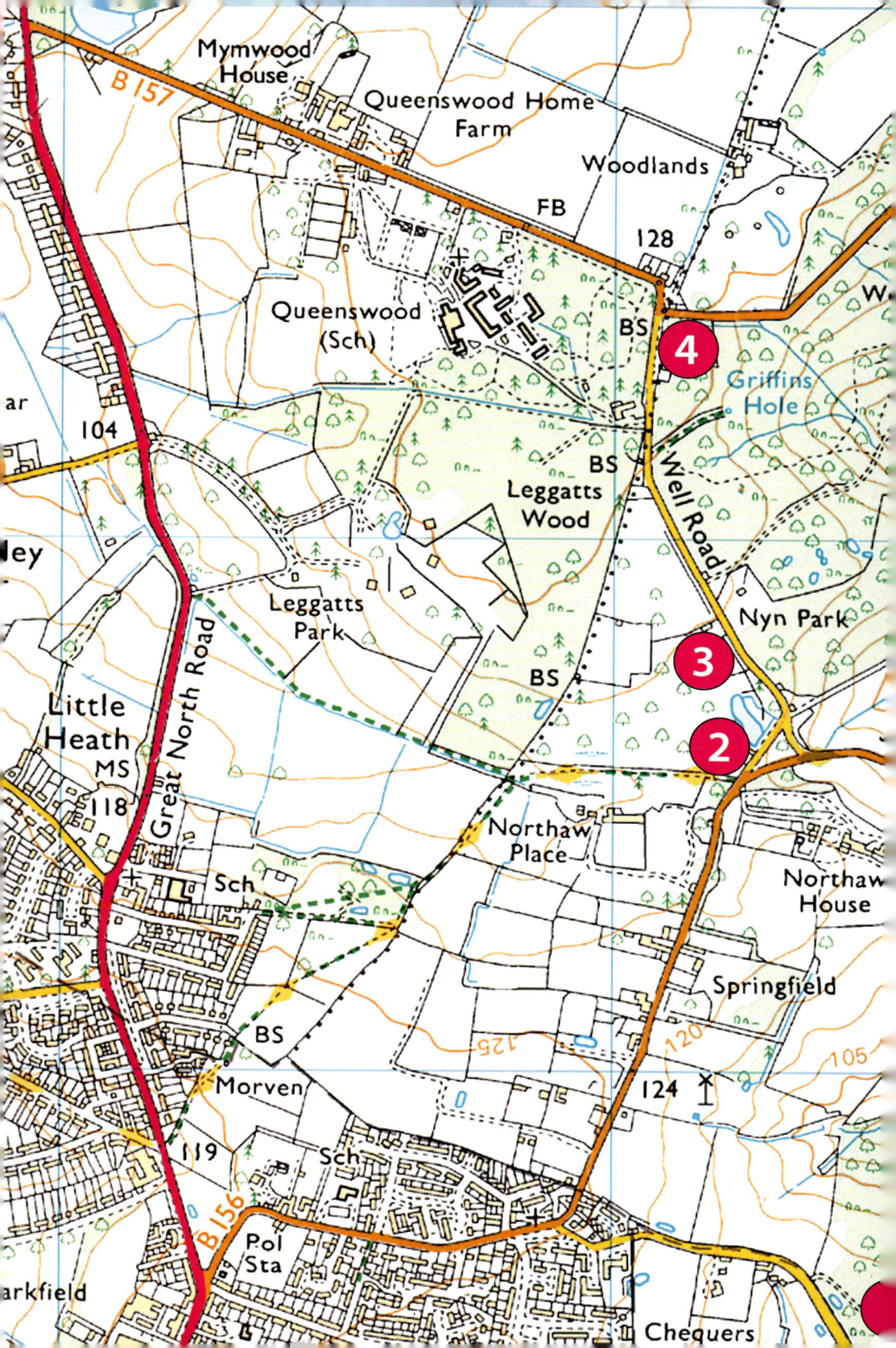

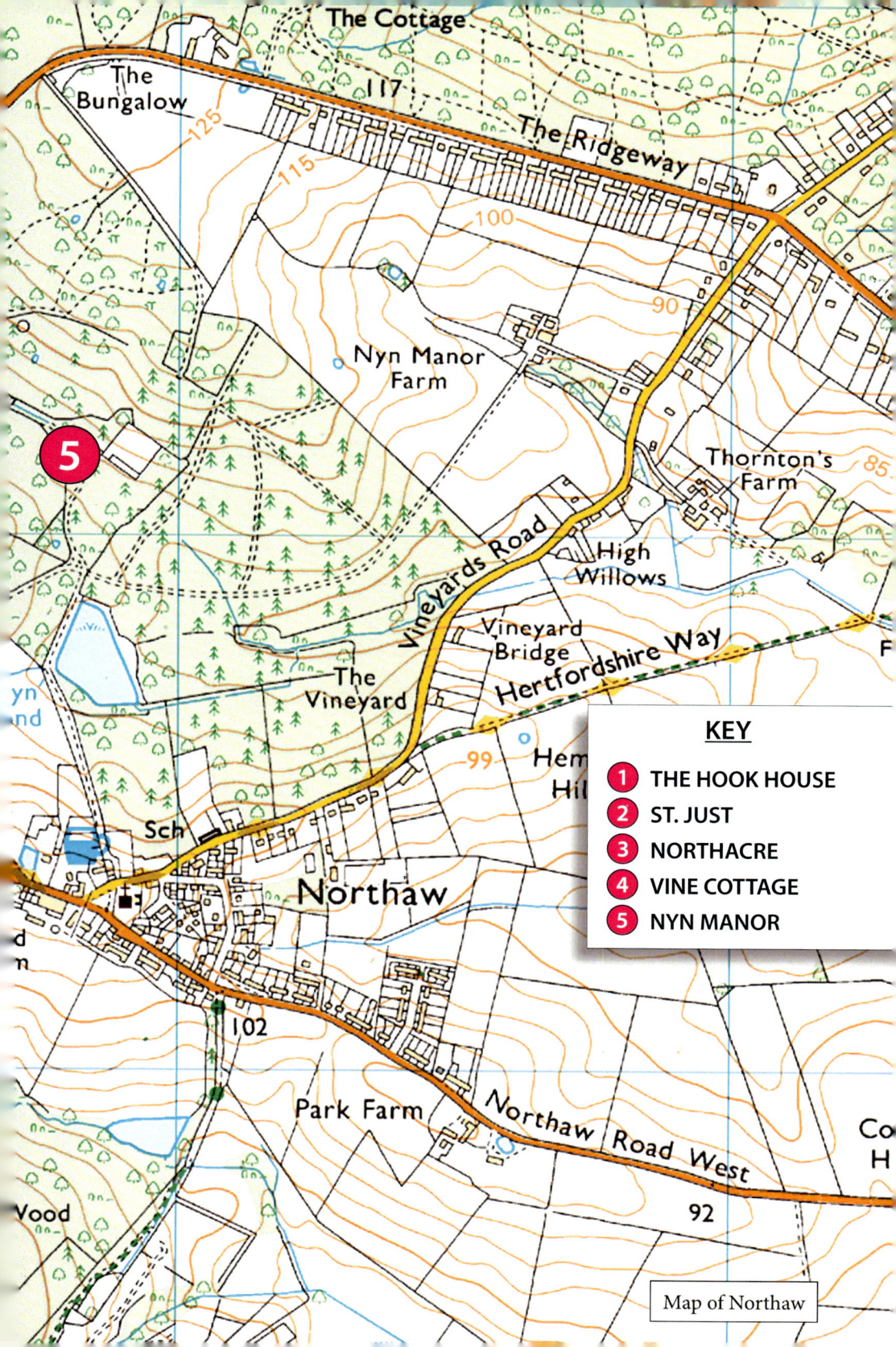

Map of Northaw

KEY

1. THE HOOK HOUSE
2. ST. JUST
3. NORTHACRE
4. VINE COTTAGE
5. NYN MANOR

NORTHAW

AND
SO MUCH MORE

Social History in Hertfordshire

PETER D WEST

CONTENTS

PHOTOGRAPHS

Introduction –
Some Families And Some Connections

The following pages in this book are not a part of my 'Family History'. They have arisen following some years spent in researching something of the history of several notable families who all had or have connections with Hertfordshire, and in particular, with Northaw. This research arose from circumstances which became apparent during a study of my own family when some quite remarkable facts materialised.

In order for these to become clear, it is necessary for me to offer a brief outline of a small part of my family.

My father, Albert Edward West, was admitted to the Infant Department of Gayhurst Road School in Dalston, Hackney, on 8th April 1907. On the same day, his cousin, Hilda Alice Pay, was admitted to the same school and they appear next to one another in the School Admissions Register.

Albert married in Northaw Parish Church, in Hertfordshire, and he and my mother lived in Tolmers Road, Cuffley, where I was born. I was baptised in the same church of St Thomas a Becket. At a later time, Albert's father and mother, and members of his family, were, and are, remembered in the family grave next to the Church in Northaw.

Clearly the West family has strong links with Northaw.

Hilda Pay, my father's cousin, married Robert Dodd and their son, Roy, was born in 'Foxholes' Nursing Home in Hitchin on 9th February 1941.

'Foxholes' was originally the home of William Tindall Lucas who, with his father, became greatly involved in the development of a bank in Hitchin. At a later stage, the Hitchin Bank joined with other smaller banks to form what was to become Barclays Bank. The bank in Hitchin was the head office of the area at the time of the amalgamation.

My father, together with other members of the West family, became prominent members of Barclays Bank in later years, as directors, managers and clerical staff.

William T Lucas sold 'Foxholes' to Philip Devitt and moved to 'The Hall' in Welwyn where he spent the rest of his life.

Philip Devitt lived in 'Foxholes' for some years before purchasing 'Northaw Place', a large estate in Northaw, in 1928.

In May 1935 Britain celebrated the Silver Jubilee of King George V and Queen Mary. As a small child, I was taken, with my cousin John Holmes, on my first visit to 'Northaw Place' where the occasion of the jubilee was being marked by Sir Phillip and Lady Devitt with a garden party. The children present were given commemorative mugs and spoons which were treasured for years to come. Sadly the King died at Sandringham just eight months later.

Previously 'Northaw Place' had been a preparatory school for boys run by the Reverend Frederic Hall and other clergymen of The Church of England. The pupils were prepared for entrance to higher levels of education, in particular to Haileybury, a well-known and highly regarded public school in Great Amwell, Hertfordshire, where their Headmaster had once taught.

I became the Headmaster of a Church of England School in North London in 1970 when I was responsible for the preparation of pupils for a variety of 'secondary experiences', including the entrance to Haileybury College and similar establishments.

'Northaw Place' was in close proximity to 'Northaw House' and the families of both were often linked together in carrying out 'good works' for the Northaw community as well as for the children of London and further afield.

Adjoining 'Northaw House' were stables and stud farm where some fine horses were bred. In later years, after my retirement from teaching, I spent much of my time visiting stud farms, yearling sales and almost every race course in the United Kingdom, having a great love of horses myself. Of course, I had only heard of the names of Jack Joel and Dorothy Paget and knew little of what took place before the Second World War in the 'Sport of Kings'. A later realisation of what had actually happened in Northaw was of great interest to me and, thankfully, the buildings where it all happened are still standing.

It was these facts, and the various family connections of people, outside of my family but within Hertfordshire, that led to the research shown in the following pages.

It has been my aim to show what the people born in, or closely connected with, one small Hertfordshire village have contributed to their society, either through education, commerce or their various churches, or through the service that they have given to the country in which they have lived.

Peter D West

1

Northaw Now

Today, Northaw is a village situated between Potters Bar and Cuffley in Hertfordshire. It is in the Welwyn/Hatfield district and the parish of Northaw and Cuffley.

The land rises and falls quite steeply around the village which is set among farmlands and streams, much of these having the background of the Great Wood. There is a lake visible from the winding road that runs like a switchback through the village. A number of large houses in the surrounding area, in Coopers Lane and Vineyards Road, catch one's attention and give the feeling of the wealth that existed in the area in days gone by.

One's attention is immediately drawn to the village green and its setting. Surrounding the village green are some small cottages and some newer, larger houses, a stud farm, the village school, the old parsonage and two inns. The small community is dominated by the Church of St Thomas a Becket with its 73ft high tower.

The two inns, 'The Sun Inn', to the west of the village green, and 'The Two Brewers' to the east, were trading at the very beginning of the 18th century and provided many of the needs of those passing through and those living in or close to Northaw village.

'The Sun' has been reduced in size and part of the original building has been turned into houses. In the 18th Century there were rooms for travellers and stabling for horses. There have been many licensees since that time and the inn remains popular to this day serving food and drink of a high quality.

'The Two Brewers' has been used for many different purposes, as well as providing sustenance. It has been the village grocery shop, the post office, and offices for a variety of functions such as tax collection. Today it serves very good meals in an attractive setting and has proved to be a very welcoming venue for many years.

The Village Green itself displays the award of Hertfordshire's Best Kept Small Village in 1999 and proudly bears the memorial for those of the armed forces from Northaw who died in the two World Wars. Of great interest is the village pump which was placed on the green, in 1862, in order to make use of the large water storage tank that was dug into the ground and fed from springs below. A further three tanks followed and supplied the village with what was thought to be pure drinking water. The covers of these tanks remain to be seen. Prior to this, the supply of water came from ponds and streams, or from 'Griffin Hole', a well or water source in Well Road, to the west of 'Nyn Hall'. A map of 1811, used to identify various properties or parish lands which were sold at auction in that year, clearly illustrates several sources of spring water in that area.

Apart from the 'Old Vicarage', formerly the parsonage, built in 1752 and situated next to the church, and 'Vernon House', built behind the 'Sun Inn', the most noticeable or influential buildings stood or stand just outside the village but, nevertheless, have played an important part in the village life. Among these were 'Nyn Hall', no longer in existence, together with 'Northaw Place' and 'Northaw House' which are still very much a part of the scene. It is the history of the families who lived in these houses that form a major part of this work.

There has been little development in and around the village during the past hundred years in comparison with both Cuffley and Potters Bar which have seen massive changes. These have taken place because of the development of the railway system that runs through both places.

In 1930 Cuffley was no bigger than Northaw but in the years that have followed, a massive residential development has taken place in and around Tolmers Road although, apart from the development of Cuffley Hall into a community area, little commercial development has taken place. However, there is an industrial development, together with large garages and showrooms, in an area close to the station, which has changed the nature of Cuffley considerably.

Potters Bar has been developed in the same way, now having industrial estates, comprehensive schools, huge concrete office blocks, large shopping areas and multiple stores. It has become a very busy town, extending over a wide area.

The 2001 census showed that the Parish of Northaw had a population of 5,190 people. Most of these lived in Cuffley. In fact, only 450 lived in Northaw village and its immediate surroundings.

There is a very real danger that the identity of Northaw may be swallowed up in the surrounding areas in the future. The aim of this book is to establish this identity and examine its history, illustrating the important part that it has played in Hertfordshire and, indeed, in our country as a whole, during the past two hundred years or more.

Northaw Church

The most noticeable building in the village is, of course, the church of St Thomas à Becket.

The Dedication of the Church suggests that it was probably built to commemorate the murder of Becket in Canterbury in 1170.

It is almost certain that a chapel, on or near the site of the present church, existed in Northaw in 1215.

A 16th Century description says that the first church was ' A rude Gothic structure, one continued building of brick and flint, having at the West End a square tower of the like materials, with only one bell in it and a weathercock.' This church was demolished in 1808 by William Strode, the Lord of The Manor, as it was felt to be inadequate for the Parish of Northaw.

A second church, built in 1810 and largely funded by Strode, was brick built, covered with stucco and roofed with slate. Internally the walls were faced with deal that was covered with sand to represent stone. Photographs show that this church had a covered walkway from the porch to the road. By 1879, it was badly in need of repair but insufficient funds could be raised for this. In 1881, it was completely destroyed by fire.

Through considerable efforts to raise money, the Reverend William Bonsey enabled the present church to be built a year later. Most of the money for the rebuilding came from John Kidston of 'Nyn Manor'.

The architects were Charles Kirk and Sons of Sleaford in Lincolnshire and it was built in thirteen months by John Bentley of Waltham Abbey with the dedication taking place on 28th September 1882.

The church is a fine example of Victorian Gothic architecture. The large stained glass windows were designed between 1886 and 1897 by Ward & Hughes and dedicated to Queen Victoria. The three stained glass windows in the north aisle are in memory of John Kidston and were presented by his wife, his nephew and his niece.

The tower, 73 feet high, has parapet walls with pierced tracery panelling and four pinnacles each 12 feet high. There are six bells at present, the largest weighing 13 cwt. and made by Taylors of Loughborough. There is a stone pulpit with a delicately carved surround of evangelists and apostles.

Between 1570 and 2010, a period of 440 years, 39 incumbents held office. There was no one in office between 1656 and 1662 or between 1691 and 1693.

The longest serving were:

Thomas Preston	1719-1769 (except 1725-1732)	43 years
John Heathfield	1769-1810	41 years
Samuel Davis	1810-1845	35 years
Max Bryant	1951-1979	28 years
John Finchback	1693-1719	26 years

Edward Kitson 1893-1914 will be seen, at a later stage, as an important link between the families of Northaw and those of Devon.

The Parsonage was built in 1752 and the Reverend Thomas Preston lived there. The succeeding vicars of Northaw lived in this building which was altered and enlarged. It is now known as the 'Old Vicarage'. It was sold and a smaller house was built for the clergy in Vineyards Road about 1933.

Not all of the clergy lived in the vicarage during all of their terms of office. In 1914 Reverend Francis Bonsey lived in a house called 'Laffords' in Northaw Road and, after nine years, the Reverend Max Bryant moved from Vineyards Road to 'Vine Cottage' until his retirement in 1979. Until very recently, 'Vine Cottage' stood at the junction of Well Road and The Ridgeway in a derelict and very poor state. This year, 2010, it is in the process of being rebuilt or refurbished, such work being almost complete.

In recent times, clergy have shared the work in the parishes of Northaw and Cuffley. The most recent to have shared this responsibility were the Reverend Michael Beer and the Reverend Ann Beer, acting as Michael's assistant. They lived in the Vicarage in Hill Rise, Cuffley.

Fewer services have taken place, compared with days gone by, and, this year, visiting clergy have covered the absence of a resident vicar. On 22nd September, 2010, a very successful service, which saw the licensing of Rachel Phillips, as priest-in-charge of Northaw and Cuffley parishes, took place in St Andrew's, Cuffley with the Bishop of St Alban's officiating.

Northaw Village

Little is known about how or when the village of Northaw was actually formed. Few references have been made to the village itself but it was undoubtedly a very gradual process. The village was not recorded in the Domesday Book.

The Manor of Northaw, which included the hamlets of Northaw and Cuffley, was granted to the Abbot and monks of St Alban's Abbey in the 8th century. It is said that a chapel was built some two hundred years later in the area where Northaw village now stands.

It is a well-known fact that the whole of this area, north of London, was covered with forest areas stretching for many miles. These were the hunting grounds used by royalty and the nobility. Palaces and hunting lodges such as 'Theobalds', 'Hatfield', 'Hunsdon' and 'Broomfield' were built in the area and royalty stayed in these to enjoy their sport.

The area where the village grew was largely woodland with some areas of heath and rough ground. It is believed that a group of people formed a small community around the chapel and gradually cleared the woodland in order to use it for farming.

The soil was heavy clay with a gravel subsoil and unsuitable for anything but the breeding of sheep and cows. Dairy farming did not begin in the area until much later.

Towards the end of the 19th Century the chief crops, recorded in the trade directories, were 'wheat, beans and roots'. Real arable farming could only take place where there was adequate drainage and where fertilisation was possible, such as in the estates of the wealthy.

The one determining factor that ensured the growth of both Northaw and Cuffley was the discovery of spring waters in the area. These waters were believed to be beneficial to healthy growth. The patronage of King James I and his court, which came from 'Theobalds' to this area, led to many people following suit in the years to come to 'take the waters'. In addition, many came to like the area and decided to build their country houses in and around Northaw from the end of the 17th century and for the next one hundred years.

'The King's Well', as it was named, as well as attracting people to the area, also brought trade to the small community that had formed, particularly to the inns in the area. Both 'The Sun Inn' and 'The Two Brewers' had opened at the beginning of the 18th Century.

It was not until the 19th Century that real changes began to take place in the village. In the first half of the century, the village itself was very largely occupied by farmers, agricultural labourers and those who, in some way, worked on the land, perhaps as woodmen, gardeners or gamekeepers. However, there was a bakery, as well as a butcher's shop and a shoe maker's, at this time.

People often took on more than one role in the village and this is well-illustrated by the licensees of 'The Two Brewers'. This inn housed the village grocery store and was also used to run a tailoring business as well as the village post office at a later date.

The Walter family, thought to have come to Northaw from London, took over the licence of the inn from the Crockford family in the middle of the 18th century.

A descendent, Charles Augustus Walter, married Mary, the daughter of John and Sarah Beck of Hatfield, in Northaw in October 1789 and their eldest son, Vincent, was born in September 1790. Vincent had a younger brother, named after his father, as well as a younger sister, Sarah, and a brother, Thomas.

Northaw Village Green

The Sun at Northaw

The Kidston Institute

The Old Bakery

The rebuilding of Nyn Hall in 2010

The rebuilding of Nyn Hall in 2010

Northaw House

Hook House

The Old Vicarage

In due course, Vincent Walter became the landlord of the inn where he organised a delivery and a receipt of mail once on each day of the week to and from Chipping Barnet. In addition he acted as the collector of assessed taxes.

Francis Walter, who came from Clerkenwell in London, was living in the village in the first half of the 19th century. He was six years older than Vincent and, although he wasn't a brother, he was, almost certainly, related to him. Francis was a journeyman tailor and lived with his wife and his cousins in a cottage in the village. There can be no doubt that he was working with other tailors from Vincent's inn.

Vincent married Sarah in 1814 and their son, William, who was born in 1822 in Northaw, married and had two children. As well as working in the grocery shop, he became the village carrier travelling to, and returning the same day, from the 'Cross Keys Inn' in St John Street, Clerkenwell, on Monday, Wednesday and Friday of each week.

At a later date, in the 1860's, William took over as licensee of the inn and his work as a carrier was taken on by Stracey Lake who travelled on Tuesdays and Fridays to the same inn while William concentrated on the grocery business. Later still, Thomas Bradfield, became the carrier and called at the 'Green Man' in Oxford Circus, London on the same days, Tuesday and Friday of each week.

In 1881, William's widow, Ann, was the licensee of 'The Two Brewers'. She was 57 and her children, William 24, Georgiana, 18 and Harry 15, all born in the village, were with her. Ann died in June, 1889 at the age of 65 and was buried in Northaw, the service being conducted by the Reverend William Bonsey.

The family continued to run the inn for some time after this. Georgiana married Henry Norris and they were recorded as the publicans at the beginning of the 20th Century.

Another family with long associations in Northaw were the Thomlinsons who ran the blacksmith's in Coopers Lane. James Thomlinson worked there for many years and was recorded in the village in 1861 at the age of 80. Another family of blacksmiths, John Taylor, aged 80, from Hatfield, and his son, John, 40, and John's wife,

Mary, from St Alban's, were also working in the village at this time.

The families in the village lived in small cottages. From the beginning of the century some parents, who sought an education for their children outside of their homes, sent them to the Parsonage. A school was run there from 1816 until 1824 when it was said to have closed. A new one was opened in Church Lane in the property of Mr Binyon who became the master.

The incumbent living in the parsonage from 1845 until 1852 was Richard Parkinson. In 1851 he was recorded as being 44 and born in Leeds. His wife, Margaret, 38 and born in Ireland, was with him and their three sons and two daughters. What is of interest is that the census shows two pupils with them, one from London and the other a British subject from the East Indies, both aged 12.

Did this mean that education was still being provided in the Parsonage, as well as in Binyon's school, and continued there until the family left at the time the new school was opened in 1852?

John Hickman Binyon was the son of William Binyon and Sarah Holworth who were married in 1793. John was born in Lidlington in Bedfordshire four years later. Several generations of this family lived in that village. John married Patty Crouch there in 1823 and they moved to Northaw. John was a farmer but also became a teacher. Their son, John Crouch Binyon, worked in the village butcher's shop for several years.

His father, as well as farming, and teaching until 1851, became clerk to the Hatfield Union, vestry clerk and superintendent registrar of births, marriages and deaths for Hatfield and Welwyn Unions.

John Binyon was still in Northaw after 50 years and living in one of his own cottages in 1871 at the age of 74. He was a widower. In order to manage the farm, his younger son, Edward Eldred Binyon, had returned to his birthplace, after marrying Rachel, born in Chelsea, and emigrating to Australia where he and his wife had three children. John's two teenage granddaughters shared his cottage with him while Edward, Rachel and their son Eldred, aged 9, were next door.

In 1852, when a new National School was built in Vineyards Road, at a cost of £600, John Binyon's school closed. The new school had places for 60 boys and girls and 40 infants. There was accommodation for a master and a mistress. This school was extended in 1879 and many additional developments have taken place since then.

Censuses show that many men were being employed in positions such as butlers or footmen, by barristers, merchants and other wealthy families. These servants were living in the larger houses that were being built while their families were living in cottages in the village. The women were also undertaking work as dressmakers, laundresses and a variety of domestic work; some travelling to the large houses from their dwellings. Other men and their families were living in cottages on the estates, rather than in those of the village. These were particularly gardeners, coachmen, grooms and gamekeepers.

More tradespersons were moving into Northaw. Bricklayers, masons, carriers and carpenters, boot and shoe makers, whitesmiths, farriers and wheelwrights, as well as the village constable, all forming a part of the community.

There were one or two unexpected residents. A Chelsea pensioner, aged 71, with his wife, aged 66 and born in Northaw, as well as an artist, with his wife and two young children who were living in Coopers Lane, next to 'Fairlawn House'.

Others were much less surprising as they had been drawn there through the development of the large country estates. It is these buildings, and the families living in them, that are considered in the following pages.

2

'Nyn Hall Palace' and Manor House

These were the first of the larger buildings of Northaw. The 450 acres of land which formed the Nyn Manor estate originally were a part of the Manor of Northaw. As stated, this land had been granted to the Abbott and monks of St Alban's in the late 8th Century. Nyn Manor was probably created after the Dissolution of the Monasteries when many of the lands belonging to the monks were divided up.

It is believed that 'Nyn Hall Palace' was built by the Earl of Warwick in the latter part of the 16th Century. This was a very large building which contained a huge dining hall, paved with marble, and having a raised platform at one end. There was also a long gallery and an impressive library. Other rooms in the house were of no great size.

The Manor passed to the Earls of Bedford in 1604 and it was sold to William Leman. His descendants, John Granger and William Strode, held the manor until 1809 when the land was broken up and sold at an auction in 1811. The land surrounding the manor house, then reduced by 200 acres, was purchased by Patrick Thompson who, in turn, sold it to the Trenchard family.

'Nyn Hall' was demolished in 1774 and a much smaller house was erected on the site. This was used by the Lords of the Manor, as stated above, for more than a hundred years until it was extended into a large Tudor style mansion, then called 'Nyn Park', which was built for John Pearson Kidston who purchased the property from the Trenchard family in 1876, together with 250 acres of land.

Mr Kidston, a merchant and shipowner, was born in Scotland in 1828, as was his wife, Janet Maitland Bruce, ten years later.

John was the son of Archibald and Janet Kidston who lived in Cambuslang, Lanarkshire, on the southern outskirts of Glasgow. Archibald, born in Nova Scotia and a British subject, was an iron and hardware merchant. He and Janet had eight children between 1820 and 1840. By 1851, he had also become a farmer of 376 acres, employing 25 labourers. Twenty years later, he and his family were still living in 'Newton House', where they had been for the past thirty years. At this time, Archibald had retired.

John, like his father, became an iron merchant and he and his wife lived in Cambuslang. They were married in Skiplaugh in the East Riding of Yorshire in 1858 when Janet was 18. In 1871 they were living in 'Cairn House' in Cambuslang when John was a ship and land owner, as well as an iron merchant.

Five years after he had purchased 'Nyn Park', John was living there with his wife, Janet, as well as two nieces and a cousin. Also living in the house were a butler, a footman, a cook and four maids. A coachman, with his family, a groom and a gardener were living in cottages in the grounds.

The house was extensive, of a Tudor style, and surrounded by immaculate lawns. Apparently, the horses that were used to pull the mowing machines wore leather boots in order to protect the grass. Croquet was played on these lawns. There was a small summer house, a stable block and a courtyard, as well as a number of very large greenhouses where John grew ferns and palms as well as varieties of Chrysanthemum to great effect. Of course, there was a huge lake which is still in existence and which has gone through many different stages of cleanliness and usefulness in its time. Inside the house on the ground floor was a great hall, a drawing room and a massive dining room. In addition there were sitting rooms, a library, and toilet facilities, as well as a large kitchen, storerooms and a scullery. There was a conservatory which led to a terrace where formal tea was served in appropriate conditions. The men wore white flannels and blazers and the ladies dressed for the occasion.

When the village church was destroyed by fire in 1881, the Kidston family donated large sums of money to enable it to be rebuilt in a truly splendid fashion. Seldom can a small village like Northaw have had such a magnificent church as St. Thomas's. The organ was presented by

Mrs Kidston in 1882, as was The Vicarage and three acres of land. In 1888 the north aisle of the church was built, again with the funding provided by John Kidston. Unlike many others, this Lord of the Manor certainly believed in the responsibilities that he had towards the community.

In 1890 Mrs Kidston, together with Miss Harriet Le Blanc ('Northaw House') who was a governor of the St Pancras Workhouse, converted 'Nyn Cottage', which stood opposite the church in Vineyards Road, into a convalescent home for destitute children. In the Summer, every fortnight, six children were brought from London for a holiday in Northaw.

Perhaps John Kidston's greatest pride and joy was his stud farm. He was one of the best-known county breeders of shire horses and spent much time in making improvements for this work. He won numerous awards for his achievement.

He died in September, 1894 at the age of 66. He was buried in Northaw on 1st October, the service being conducted by the Reverend Edward B. B. Kitson. His widow continued to live in 'Nyn Park'.

In 1904 the 'Kidston Institute' in Northaw Road was built by Mrs Kidston as a social centre for men, having a reading room or club which was subject to certain rules and regulations. She also donated £1,000 to be invested, with the income to be used for the upkeep of the institute as long as it existed. It is still used at present.

In 1917 Mrs Kidston, with Miss Le Blanc and Miss Poland (see Hall and Poland families), formed the first Women's Institute in Hertfordshire.

Janet Kidston died at the age of 90 and was buried in Northaw on 5th December, 1929. The Reverend Edward Allen conducted the service in the Parish Church.

Following Mrs Kidston's death, 'Nyn Park' was sold to a Mrs Arthur who, in turn, moved to 'Vernon House' in the village in 1947. At this point the property was sold to St Bartholomew's Hospital when it was used for the storage of beds and furniture. Originally it was planned to use the property for convalescence but this did not happen.

A second film adaptation of 'Night Must Fall', a play written by Emlyn Williams in 1935, was filmed in 'Nyn Park' and in Northaw in 1946 and starred Albert Finney, Susan Hampshire and Sheila Hancock.

On Good Friday in 1963 the house was reduced to a ruin by fire when the caretaker was away. This must have accounted for the devastation, as the fire was allowed to spread throughout the buildings until the breaking of timbers was heard in the village. It is understood that fire fighters had great difficulty in reaching the scene because of the thick mud that surrounded the house. Certainly there was a change from earlier days.

In 1968, the estate was purchased by a Major Frank Russell Dore who was a keen silviculturist. He achieved a great deal in restoring much of the woodland areas of the park, as well as introducing new and rare trees. He and his wife lived in 'Well House' which was a weather-boarded house with a tiled roof and was situated on the Hatfield driveway of the old house. It is a condition that 'Well House' will be destroyed should another house be built to replace 'Nyn Park'.

Major Dore died in May 1987. His estate was valued at £3,169,777. After making provision for his wife in her lifetime, he bequeathed the Nyn estate to Haileybury and the Imperial Service Colleges. In 1997 it was sold to make improvements to the colleges.

The park, with planning permission to build a new house in 250 acres of land, was offered for sale at a figure of around £10,000,000 in 2009. Building work started in that year and is progressing well in 2010. The building, a project under construction by Julian Bicknell Associates of London, is on behalf of Bessington Investments Limited of Jersey.

The occupant of the new house will not be disclosed in spite of numerous enquiries to all of the appropriate sources. It is probable that such information will be revealed within the next two years!

3

'Northaw House'

'Northaw House' was formerly known as 'Nyn Lodge'. It was built in 1698 for a Mrs Angin.

In 1741 it was occupied by a Lord Mayor of London, Sir Samuel Pennant, who was also the Lord of the Manor.

Samuel was a member of the very wealthy Pennant family who made a fortune from Jamaican sugar and Welsh slate and who, at one time, lived in the north of Wales in the Whitford/Holywell area. At a later date, from 1820 until 1845, the family built 'Penrhyn Castle', near Bangor, with views of Snowdonia. Originally a medieval, fortified manor house, it stood on a site of 40,000 acres. It was twice rebuilt before a country house, in the form of a Norman Castle, was constructed at a cost of about £150,000. (Today's equivalent would be approximately £49,000,000).

Samuel's nephew, Richard, became the 1st Baron Penrhyn. The castle and grounds now belong to the National Trust as it was accepted by the government in lieu of death duties.

Samuel Pennant became an alderman of the City of London in 1745, representing the Bishopsgate ward. He was also the MP for Liverpool and was elected as Lord Mayor of London in 1749.

One of the duties of the Lord Mayor was to preside over the Court sitting in the Sessions House, next to Newgate Prison. Previously trials had taken place in the prison where conditions were so bad that 'jail fever' had led to the deaths of both prisoners and court officials. In spite of the move outside, the fever, now identified as Typhus Fever, struck again, being carried into the court by prisoners. As a result, the Lord Mayor, two judges, an alderman, an under sheriff and between fifty and sixty court officials died.

Samuel Pennant lost his life before the completion of his term of office as Lord Mayor. A new election had to take place in subdued circumstances and with much sadness.

The new mayor following Samuel Pennant was John Blachford.

John was born in 1682, the fourth son of Captain Robert Blachford and Elizabeth (née Mann), in Sandhill Manor. He was baptised in Fordingbridge, Hampshire. At the age of 18 he was sent to London to work as an apprentice goldsmith. He prospered in his work and gained his 'freedom by service' in 1710. He worked successfully as a goldsmith in London and, in 1728, bought Bowcombe Manor, near Carrisbrooke, on the Isle of Wight.

In 1744 he became Prime Warden of the Goldsmith's Company and an alderman of the Cripplegate area of London. He was a governor of St Bartholomew's Hospital in London and became its President in 1754.

He spent his later years at 'Nyn Lodge' ('Northaw House'), following in the footsteps of Samuel Pennant. He died there in September, 1759 at the age of 77 and was buried in the centre aisle towards the west end of the Parish Church. His memorial stone, last seen in 1840, was lost in the rebuilding of the church following the fire of 1881.

The new 'Northaw House' was built from 1774 onwards, using brickwork from the demolished Nyn Hall.

In 1805 William Strode lived there. (see Nyn Hall) He demolished all the surrounding houses to create a park around this new house. One of those demolished was 'Muscombes' where he had lived for sixteen years before. Others were 'Goat House', 'Gouldings' and the 'Steward's House'. Shortly after this he organised the pulling down of the first parish church.

At the auction in 1811 the house was sold to Sir Simon Le Blanc, a Judge of The King's Bench, and it remained in the Le Blanc Family until 1896.

It is said that at the time Sir Simon bought 'Northaw House', the lane from the village ran in a straight line to Coopers Lane, passing close to his property. Disturbed by the noise made by passing villagers, Sir Simon sought to have the lane made into a more circuitous route. Apparently, this was done and was named 'Judge's Hill'. Apart from the fact that the road is now some distance from 'Northaw House' and is certainly a winding and hilly route, having the name that it does, no hard evidence can be found of this story. Early maps show what was probably the lane in question.

On the 1861 Census, Charles William Faber, an eminent barrister, was in residence with his family, as, indeed, he was on the 1871 Census. Obviously, Mr Faber was a lessee of the Le Blanc family.

Charles Faber was described as a landed proprietor, and born in Yorkshire. In 1861, he and his wife had three sons and three daughters and, by 1871, another son had been born. At this time they employed a governess, a cook, two nurses, four maids and a coachman.

The 1881 Census recorded the Le Blanc Family living in 'Northaw House'. Thomas Le Blanc, a retired military officer, born in Guernsey, was 72. His wife, 56, was born in Tewkesbury in Gloucestershire. They employed a butler, a cook, a footman and three maids.

Captain Le Blanc was recorded as being in residence at the House in 1891 when a gardener and a groom had been added to the Staff.

He died in November, 1896. The funeral service was conducted by the Reverend Bonsey who had left Northaw earlier to become the Vicar of Lancaster by this time. Thomas was buried in Northaw as were other members of the le Blanc family who moved to Bournemouth. Henry le Blanc, who died at the age of 55, was buried in 1910 and Janet, who had lived at 'Nyn Park', died aged 74 and was brought back to Northaw in 1930. The family graves are in the north east corner of the churchyard.

The house was sold and a Horse Racing Stud was established there under the ownership of Jack Joel.

The 1901 Census recorded only a housekeeper and servants at the property.

Subsequently, in 1922 Reginald Gardiner Heaton was recorded at Northaw. He employed a groom, John Henry Marshall, and a gardener, Harry Ebbs.

Baron, Lord Woolavington, was shown there in 1929. His other addresses were 25 Berkeley Square W1 and the Carlton, Conservative and Jockey Clubs in London. Harry Ebbs was the gardener at Northaw.

By 1933 Lord Woolavington's addresses were Lavington Park, Petworth in Sussex, Grove House in Newmarket, Suffolk, and Knockando in Morayshire as well as his property in Berkeley Square and his clubs in London. Harry Ebbs was still the gardener!

But who was Harry Ebbs and why was he an important player in the history of Northaw?

By about 1937 the Hon. Dorothy Paget was living at Northaw.

These connections ceased in 1940 and 'Northaw House' was used as a Children's Hospital from 1943 until 1970 when it became office accommodation in later years. It remains as the offices of an Architects' Partnership in 2010. The Northaw Stud is no longer a part of 'Northaw House' and is run as a quite separate enterprise, having little connection with horse racing.

As stated, 'Northaw House' and the Stud Farm were of great importance to several families. In the following pages some brief notes have been made about them:

Lord Woolavington
Jack Barnato Joel
Dorothy Paget
Harry Ebbs

Baron Woolavington

The first Baron Woolavington was born James Buchanan in 1849 in Ontario, Canada, the son of Scottish immigrant parents who returned to the United Kingdom shortly after his birth. He was brought up in Larne in Scotland where he was educated privately as he suffered from ill-health.

As a young man he joined a Glasgow shipping firm and worked as an office boy. He worked his way up to becoming a customs clerk before deciding, at the age of nineteen, to join his brother, William, a grain merchant in Glasgow. Later he tried, unsuccessfully, to work on his own in Scotland.

However, he realised that there was a market for Scottish whisky in England and, at the age of thirty, he moved to London, where he worked as an agent for Charles Mackinlay & Co.

Five years later, he started his own business and produced his own, Buchanan Blend, of whisky. James built his business to form a private limited company and was outselling his competitors by the time he was sixty.

In 1910 he attempted an amalgamation with Dewars and Walkers but was unsuccessful. In 1915 he joined with Dewars to form Scottish Whisky Brands Ltd which was renamed Buchanan Dewar Ltd before another amalgamation with the Distillers Company took place.

At the age of 42, he married a nurse, thirteen years younger than he. They had a daughter and a son who died in infancy. During the First World War, his wife nursed the wounded in London hospitals. She died suddenly in October, 1918.

James had many interests outside of the whisky business, including breeding cattle, sheep and horses. He also enjoyed hunting and salmon fishing. Perhaps his greatest love was the breeding of thoroughbred horses.

He bought Lavington Park in Sussex. Today, the park, situated in East Lavington, is really an extension to the village of Graffham, some five miles south of Petworth.

This was an estate of 3000 acres. Here he created an exceptional stud farm. It became one of Britain's longest-established stud farms and was set in a beautiful location at the foot of the South Downs.

James and his family lived in a large manor house, built higher on the downs and overlooking his large estate and the village below.

He was appointed High Sheriff of Sussex in 1910 and was created a baronet in 1920. He became Baron Woolavington in 1922.

He was one of the top owner/breeders of his time and won the St Leger in 1916 with a horse named 'Hurry On' who sired his Derby winners in 1922 and 1926. 'Coronach' which he bred and owned won the Derby and the St Leger in 1926.

He was elected to the Jockey Club in 1927 and, in 1929, he lived in 'Northaw Place' in Hertfordshire. He was appointed GCVO in 1931.

He donated very large sums of money for the development of the

Middlesex and London Hospitals and for the restoration of St George's Chapel, Windsor, as well as to the West of Scotland Agricultural College and the Licensed Victuallers' School and Benevolent Institution.

After he died at Lavington Park in 1935, just short of his 86th birthday, his estate was estimated to have a gross value of over £7,000,000.

Both James and his wife, Anne, were buried in a separate, flint-walled garden outside of Graffham Church. Inside the church is a plaque commemorating the life of James, his good works and his care for the well-being and happiness of others.

The main house was sold but the stud was retained and remains a family business run by his grandson and great-grandson. Between 1903 and 2007, 686 winners of 2,013 races were bred at Lavington.

The stud farm, with accommodation for those working there, and stable blocks are set in two locations in a beautiful setting. Yearlings can be seen enjoying outstanding facilities.

At the present time, when members of the family visit the stud, they stay at a house in Graffham.

East Lavington house has now become Seaford College. The college was established in 1946 after its original site in Seaford, on the Sussex coast, was requisitioned by the government during the Second World War.

The houses in the grounds, formerly used by the Buchanan family's staff and 'villagers' are now a part of the college. The church, which adjoined the house, has now become the college chapel and the extensive grounds below have been converted into a variety of pitches on which various sports are played.

There is a golf course with practice greens and a driving range, a well-stocked lake for fishing, as well as facilities for archery, shooting and swimming, tennis and squash.

Approximately six hundred students, day pupils as well as weekly and full-time boarders, between the ages of seven and eighteen, attend the college and there are over one hundred members of staff.

The Joel Family – Childwickbury, the Maple Family and the Kubricks

Isaac 'Jack' Joel, a broker, born in 1802, and Rebecca Solomon, his wife, lived in Sandys Row, Spitalfields. Their first child, Coleman, was born in 1831 when Rebecca was a young teenager. They had five more children before Rebecca died in 1842, still in her 20s. Isaac married again and his wife, Elizabeth, was widowed when he died in 1847.

Elizabeth, born in 1802, looked after the shop in Sandys Row together with Isaac's children, Coleman, Sarah, Mary and Joel. Rebecca's two youngest children were no longer there in 1851.

Young Joel became a cigar maker and married Catherine Isaacs, the daughter of Isaac Isaacs and Leah Harris. They lived in the same house as Catherine's widowed father at 8 Sandys Row. Isaac had four more children living with him.

Joel, later described as a general dealer, and Catherine had three sons, Isaac, Woolf and Solomon. In 1871 they were living at 'The King of Prussia' in Middlesex Street, Whitchapel. Catherine's brother, Henry Isaacs, was the publican and Catherine was a barwoman.

Catherine's brother, Barnett Isaacs, known as Barney Barnato, encouraged his nephews to seek their fortunes in the diamond business in Kimberley, South Africa.

Barnato was extremely successful in making a fortune there. At one time he rivalled Cecil Rhodes in the diamond mining industry. Later he and Cecil became colleagues, joining together in forming De Beers Consolidated Mines in 1888.

The youngest of the brothers, Solomon, certainly made a fortune throughout a long career in Barnato Brothers and De Beers Consolidated Mines from 1901 until his death in 1931.

The dealings of the brothers were by no means straightforward and are too complex to record in this context. However, 'Solly' was given a two year prison sentence, commuted to a fine through the influence of Barney Barnato. Barney fell overboard, or may have committed suicide, while on a sea trip in 1897 and, in the following year, Solly's brother, Woolf, was shot dead in their office in Johannesburg during a dispute over allegations of blackmail.

The lives of Solomon and his older brother, Isaac, known as Jack, followed similar lines in respect of their trading in diamonds and gold. Both made absolute fortunes. Jack's time in Kimberley was cut short when he was arrested for illicit diamond buying. He jumped bail of £4000 and returned discreetly and hastily to England. Once there he joined his uncle in the London business of Barnato Brothers. He became the head of 'Johnnies' in London and was chairman after Solomon's death in 1931. 'Johnnies' was the Johannesburg Consolidated Investment Company Ltd formed by the brothers and was involved in mining, breweries and collieries in South Africa.

Both Solomon and Jack shared a love of the theatre and of horse racing. Solomon managed several London theatres and was particularly interested in Drury Lane Theatre. He had a private box in most of the larger London theatres. He married an actress, Ellen Ridley. They had three sons and two daughters. The couple separated and, after Ellen's death in 1919, Solomon married a widow who had been a child actress, Mrs Phoebe Benjuta, with whom he had one daughter. He entertained lavishly both in London at his mansion in Great Stanhope Street and in his country estates, and was a generous benefactor to the Middlesex Hospital and the National Playing Fields Association.

Solomon and Jack were extremely successful with racing and breeding and their horses won almost every important contest in the Racing Calendar.

Solomon won the Ascot Gold Cup, with Bachelor Button in 1906. This was his first big success. By 1921 he headed the list of winning owners. He had stables close to his mansion and very large estate at Maiden Erlegh.

This was situated at Earley on the outskirts of Reading and has a history covering centuries. The manor was purchased in 1878 by the Master of the South Berkshire Hunt who constructed a race course there where hunt and yeomanry races took place until the time of the First World War. The racecourse was demolished and the grandstand which previously stood there was re-erected at Newbury race course.

The estate was acquired by Solomon Joel in 1903. The house had over seventy rooms, fifty of them bedrooms, to which he added a swimming pool, built with Italian marble and painted with nude frescoes, at a cost of £12,000. The estate, with rose gardens and terraces, contained an aviary, a polo ground, tennis courts and a cricket field. It is said that many of 'Solly's' legendary parties took place there. After his death, the estate was sold and the house was found to be unsatisfactory in its use as a boys' school and a training college. After a short while the county council decided not to purchase it for council offices and it was demolished in 1960.

Solomon also owned a stud farm near Marefield in Reading. This changed its name from 'New Farm' to 'Home Stud Farm'. When Solomon died, the property was purchased and continued as a stud until the 1980s.

He leased Moulton Paddocks, just outside of Newmarket. This was originally a stud farm which was developed into one of England's most famous sporting estates. Godolphin leased the estate from 1995 and trained their horses there, bringing them from Dubai where they had spent the winter season. The very large mansion was demolished when Godolphin bought the property from the Embiricos family in 2004. It is now the centre of Godolphin Racing in this country.

As well as Moulton Paddocks, Solomon used Sefton Lodge, situated in Bury Road, Newmarket. The property is thought to have been built in 1872 and further extensions were made in a similar style after 1883 for the Duchess of Montrose, a notable racehorse owner and patroness of horse racing. The property was owned by the Joel family from 1905 until 1982 when further additions were made. In more recent times it was used by the trainer, David Loder, who had 45 successes from there in his first year of training, many trained for Sheikh Mohammed.

The house, set in 2.4 acres of land, is an exceptional example of a 19th century racing establishment, having at least 12 bedrooms, bathrooms and luxurious reception areas, as well as office accommodation. There is a trainer's house and a head lad's flat. The training facilities are first-class and include 45 stables in close proximity to Lond Hill training facilities and gallops. Today its value is thought to be in the region of £4,000,000.

Solomon's stables rivalled those of the Aga Khan, Lord Derby and Lord Astor. Jack Joel's horses were trained at Wantage and Foxhill but his studs were at Northaw and at Childwickbury near St Albans.

As an owner and breeder, he was hugely successful, winning the 1000 Guineas twice, the 2000 Guineas once and the Derby twice, with Sunstar in 1911 and with Humorist in 1921. He won the Oaks four times and the St Leger twice, as well as the Coronation Cup at Epsom. These successes were between 1903 and 1921. He was Champion Owner on three occasions.

Jack married Edith 'Fanny' Richards, born in Soho in 1866. They had three children, Kathleen, May and Joel, known as Harry and later called 'Jim'. The children were born in the district of Paddington. The 1901 census records the family at 'The Firs' in Shoot Up Hill, West Hampstead. They employed a governess, a butler, a cook and four maids. There was a coach house, with rooms over, used as living quarters for the coachman and four stablemen.

After Edith's death, Jack married the widow, Mrs Olive Coulson, nee Sopwith. Olive, born in London in 1877, and fifteen years younger than Jack, was the daughter of Thomas Sopwith. 'Tommy' Sopwith was, and is, of course, a legend in British history. His achievements in the aircraft industry, yachting and motor racing were, and remain, sensational. He was a celebrated competitor in all of these fields.

As a pioneer in English aviation, he produced the 'Sopwith Camel' aircraft which was a definitive factor in the British 'success' of World War 1, while his firm, which became Hawker Aircraft, produced the 'Hurricane', partly instrumental in winning the Battle of Britain. 'Hawker' became 'Hawker Siddeley' and was a pioneer in the production of the jet engine. Tommy was made a CBE in 1918 and was knighted in 1953. He died in 1989 at the age of 101. Needless to say, there was a 'fly past' at his funeral!

Jack Joel's horses were trained at Wantage by Charles Morton. In 1902 Jack bought a horse named 'Sundridge' at the Newmarket Sales. The horse had won four races as a three-year old and three as a four-year old but was not considered to be a classic contender. Joel paid £1,450 for him. In his fifth year the horse won five out of seven races and was sprinting in top form. At the end of his racing, 'Sundridge' had won seventeen races from thirty five starts between the ages of two to six years. Joel retired him to his Northaw stud where he stood for the next three breeding seasons.

Jack moved from Northaw when he purchased the Childwickbury estate in 1906, and 'Sundridge'was moved there.

The Childwickbury estate is situated between St Alban's and Harpenden and, again, was the property of the abbot and monks of St Alban's Abbey until the 13th century. It was acquired by the Lomax family about 1666 when the Manor House was built. One of the family, Joshua Lomax, became MP for St Alban's in 1708. The property remained in the family for nearly two hundred years.

In 1854, it was sold to Henry Heyman Toulmin, a wealthy ship owner, who was born in Hackney in 1808. He and his wife, Sarah, also from Hackney, were living at Childwickbury in 1861, having lived previously in Clapton and Havering. By this time their eldest daughter, Helen, and their eldest son, Henry, were no longer living with them.

Henry became High Sheriff of Hertfordshire.

When Henry found that the tenants on his estate were reluctant to walk the long distance to a church in St Alban's, he provided them with their own church, designed by Sir Gilbert Scott, a family friend and prominent architect of the time. It was built in 1867. This was St Mary's Church in Childwick Green, the tiny hamlet built on the estate for the workers. Henry was appointed as a lay reader by the bishop and was able to conduct simple morning and evening services. He also built a schoolroom next to the church where he and his wife held a night school to teach their tenants, some quite elderly people, how to read and write. In addition to this building, Henry also enlarged the manor house by adding two wings to the property.

On the green, outside the village church, there stands the remains of the 'village well' as is the case in Northaw. 'Childwick' means 'the dwellings by the well' and, this appears to be entirely appropriate in this instance.

At the beginning of 1871, Henry and Sarah, remained in residence in Childwick, with two sons, a daughter-in-law and two granddaughters. Later in the year Henry died. In due course, the property was inherited by his eldest son, Henry Joseph Toulmin.

Henry J. Toulmin was born in 1837 in Dalston. As a young man, he joined the Army and became a Lieutenant in the Dragoon Guards. He married Emma Louisa and their first child, Emma, was born in Brighton. Henry was 26 and his wife was 19. In 1868 and 1870, two more daughters were born at Childwick. Following this the family purchased a manor house, The Pre, just outside St Alban's on the road to Redbourn. The property, on a large estate, was once a Benedictine Nunnery. Henry's only son, Henry Wroughton Toulmin, and two more daughters were born there, the youngest being born in 1875. Two more daughters were born in Childwick, in 1878 and 1880, after he had inherited the estate. He and Emma decided to return to The Pre and, soon after this, three more daughters were born.

The Childwickbury estate was bought by Sir John Blundell Maple of the well-known upholstery, furniture and furnishing firm of Tottenham Court Road in London. His London property was in Carlton Terrace in Regent's Park. He was a member of the Carlton Club as well as St Stephen's Club.

Sir John was a horse-racing enthusiast whose horses were trained at Falmouth House and stables in Newmarket, which he bought in 1888, thought to be for £5,000, formerly the home of the famous jockey, Fred Archer, who had built the house in 1882. Tragically, after the death of his wife, Archer committed suicide in 1884.

After acquiring Childwick Manor, Sir John built Childwick Stud and Childwick Hall on the estate and he turned this into a very successful horse-breeding operation before it was purchased by Jack Joel. Sir John invested in the land surrounding the manor and doubled the size of the estate during his time there to 1749 acres. He enlarged both the church and the schoolroom which was used until 1925 and was re-opened for evacuees during World War II.

He died in November 1903, at the age of 58, and was interred in the family vault in St Mary's churchyard which contained the coffins of his daughters who died in early childhood. Lady Maple sold the estate, including the stud farm, to Jack Joel at an auction in 1906.

In 1908, a 'Sundridge' colt, 'Sunstar', was born. 'Sunstar' proved to be Joel's greatest breeding success as it went on to win the 2000 Guineas and the Derby in 1911.

'Sundridge' was sold to a French syndicate, a move which Jack lived to regret. He had a great affection for this horse, as with the others in his care. He tried to buy him back but was unsuccessful until 1920 when the horse was returned to Childwickbury. Three years later, following an attack of paralysis, the horse died at the age of 25 and was buried at the stud, next to Sunstar's dam, 'Dorris'. 'Sunstar' was retired to the stud and was highly effective in producing some fine horses, notably 'Jest', the winner of the 1000 Guineas and the Oaks in 1913 and 'Black Jester' the winner of the St Leger in the following year.

While being a very hard business man, Jack showed again that he had a great love for his horses. After winning the 1921 Derby, his horse, 'Humorist', suffered a serious lung haemorrhage and died immediately. Jack was distraught. 'Humorist's jockey was Steve Donoghue who won the Derby in the following two years. He was the leading flat race jockey in the 1910s and 1920s and was champion jockey for 10 successive years from 1914 to 1923.

When Jack's trainer, Charles Morton, retired in 1924, he was succeeded by a former assistant, Charles Peck, who had trained Solomon's horses at Isley before transferring to the stable in Newmarket. Jack moved from his Wantage stables in Berkshire to the Foxhill Stables near Swindon.

Jack's wife, Olive, died in 1937 and Jack died on 13th November three years later.

Both he and Solomon, who died at Moulton, Newmarket, in 1931 were buried with other members of the family at Willesden cemetery in London.

Jack's son, Harry 'Jim' Joel, took over his father's estate in 1940 and he too became a very highly rated owner and breeder and maintained the property for 38 years. Jim and his father were among the most successful British owner/breeders for almost the whole of the 20th century. They had 1,696 winners.

In the mid-1970s, Jim decided that he would move from the Childwick Bury manor house into Childwick Hall where the main stud buildings were situated.

In 1978 the manor house and the estate of 1100 acres were bought by a landed property company and were put up for sale in lots at an auction held in St Alban's.

The advertisement in The Times on 28th June described the Manor House as having twelve reception rooms, eighteen bedrooms with dressing rooms, eleven staff bedrooms and ten bathrooms. There was garaging with a flat, an estate office and a dairy house standing in nineteen acres of land. The estate included farms standing in seven hundred and twenty four acres. There were one hundred and forty six acres of timbered parkland and thirty seven acres of commercial woodland. There was an old mill and a number of houses and cottages formed part of the estate.

Some of the farm lands and estate houses were sold to private buyers at the auction held in St Alban's.

Stanley and Christiane Kubrick

The American film director, producer, writer and photographer of motion pictures Stanley Kubrick, born in Manhattan in July 1926, and famous for such films as 'A Clockwork Orange', '2001: A Space Odyssey', 'The Shining', 'Full Metal Jacket' and, not least, 'Barry Lyndon', surely one of the most beautiful pieces of cinematography ever produced, bought the manor house.

He moved to Childwick Bury from his property, 'Abbots Mead' in Barnet Lane, close to Elstree and Borehamwood, where he had worked in the film studios and the surrounding area since 1965.

'Abbots Mead' had been purchased from a very prosperous estate agent and quantity surveyor, later an EMI executive, the father of Simon Cowell, the well-known TV personality of Pop Idol and The X Factor.

Kubrick was seen as something of a recluse when he moved to Childwickbury Manor. Apparently, he would no longer use aeroplanes and his chauffeur driven car was limited to a speed of 30 mph at all times. He lived in the manor until his death in 1999 when he suffered a coronary thrombosis, just a short time after the release of his film 'Eyes Wide Shut' which starred Tom Cruise and Nicole Kidman. He was buried in the grounds of the manor. Kubrick's work was original, provocative, and visionary and he will always have a special place in the history of the cinema as well as in the history of Hertfordshire.

His widow, Christiane, still lives in the manor house and is much involved in Arts Festivals which are held in the grounds at Childwick on a regular basis. An exhibition of Kubrick's work was mounted in St Alban's Museum during the Summer of 2010. This was followed by an Arts Fair, held in July in the manor house grounds and stable blocks.

It was organised by Christiane Kubrick and involved the active participation of many artists, demonstrating the making of jewellery and ceramics, of wood carving, print making and glasswork. A Christmas Market, offering artistic gifts as presents, will be held at the end of November, 2010.

Christiane was born in Braunschweig, some thirty kilometres east of Hanover. Her parents were both opera singers and she was brought up in the world of the theatre. From an early age she was involved in 'dressing up', writing stories, producing puppet shows and making and playing the roles. Much of her time has always been spent in drawing and painting.

After a boarding school education at 'Salem' near Lake Constance on the Swiss/German border, she began to earn a living in the theatre.

Her career led to her working in operettas and ballet before moving into radio, theatre, TV and film. She was seen acting on German Television by Stanley Kubrick who contacted her and offered her a role in his film 'Paths of Glory' which was being made in Munich. They were married two years later.

Christiane has never stopped painting and her work has been exhibited and sold all over the world. When she is not painting she works on her creation of a puppet theatre. She makes large puppets, at once both imaginary and unusually realistic, which produce a conflict of emotions, and which ask questions as do her paintings which, while of a realistic nature, often contain unexpected and sometimes disturbing elements seen from unusual perspectives.

After Jim Joel died in 1992 at the age of 97, the Childwick Stud, together with Childwick Hall and Hedges Farm, was sold to a company headed by the Marquesa de Moratella, an owner and breeder, particularly well-known in France, but also a very successful competitor in the world of horse racing in this country.

The Paget Family and 'Camfield Place',
Beatrix Potter, Barbara Cartland

Dorothy Wyndham Paget was born in February 1905 at 32 Green Street in Mayfair. She was the second daughter of Lord Queenborough and Pauline Payne, the daughter of the American politician, William C Whitney, who was at one time Secretary of the US Navy.

Dorothy's father, Almeric Hugh Paget, one of fourteen children, was born in 1861, the son of General Lord Alfred Paget and grandson of the first Marquess of Anglesey who commanded the British Cavalry at Waterloo. Almeric left Harrow School in 1879 and moved to Iowa in the American mid-west where he spent his time herding cattle (known as a cow-puncher). Later he moved to Minnesota where he sold real estate and made a fortune. His brother introduced him into New York Society where he met his first wife, Pauline. In 1901 they returned to England.

He and Pauline had two daughters. The elder, Olive, was born in 1899 and married three times, finally becoming the wife of Sir Adrian William Maxwell Baillie, 6th Baronet and living in Leeds Castle. The second, Dorothy, was born in 1905 and remained single.

Almeric had considerable business interests in America and was a director in several commercial concerns there. He became Governor of Guy's Hospital in London, a member of the Council of the Royal Zoological Society and President of the Royal Society of St George.

He became very involved in politics and was President of the National Union of Conservative and Unionist Associations and was MP for Cambridge Borough from 1910 to 1917.

He was created Baron Queenborough of Queenborough in Kent in 1918 and was made a Knight of the Grand Cross of the British Empire in 1926.

Pauline died in 1916 and, five years later, Almeric married Edith Starr of New York. They had three daughters before Edith, a writer, died in Paris in 1933. Almeric was a keen all-round sportsman, being particularly involved in yachting and horse-racing.

As stated above, Dorothy's mother died when her daughter was still a child and, no doubt, this played a part in her becoming a badly behaved and spoilt child. She was expelled from six schools, the first of these was Heathfield School in Ascot. Eventually, she was sent to Paris where she finished her education in an establishment run by a Russian émigré.

She is said to have inherited her wealth from her maternal grandmother (Oxford DNB) which enabled her to undertake expensive leisure activities. At the age of 26 she supported the motor racing team, which won Le Mans in 1929, to the extent of £32,000. She had a love of fast driving. She was also talented in the world of show-jumping and her love of horses led to her gaining notable success in horse racing in the 1940s and 50s.

As well as owning racehorses, she bred and trained them, and certainly used the Northaw Stud for this purpose while living in

'Northaw House'. She had one thousand five hundred and thirty two winners and, of these, seven were winners of the Cheltenham Gold Cup. Five in succession were won by 'Golden Miller', who also won the Grand National for her. She twice won the Champion Hurdle and a wartime Derby in 1943 with 'Straight Deal'. She was the leading National Hunt owner in 1940/1 and 1951/2.

Records in the ODNB state that her racing cost her over £3 million. This was in addition to vast gambling losses. Her largest recorded bet was £160,000 to win £20,000. This she won. Often she did not.

She weighed twenty stones and cared nothing for her appearance. She was frequently unapproachable and could be extremely rude. She was superstitious, with a particular aversion to the colour green, which may account for her frequently being dressed in a very large speckled blue tweed overcoat.

In the afternoon of 9th February 1960, twelve days before her 55th birthday, she was found to have died from heart failure, possibly brought about by her excessive weight and the fact that she smoked a hundred cigarettes a day.

She was, of course, one of the most famous figures of Horse Racing in the first half of the 20th Century, both eccentric and formidable, one of the real characters of racing. Despite her gambling, her estate was valued at nearly £4,000,000. This was reduced to £736,000 by duties and was inherited by her sister, Lady Baillie, to whom she had rarely spoken in the latter part of her life.

Dorothy's father, Almeric Paget, had died at his home, Camfield Place, in Essendon, near Hatfield in Hertfordshire at the age of 88.

Camfield Place was an estate with a Tudor Manor House. This was pulled down in 1867 by the grandfather of Beatrix Potter, the world famous author of many children's books and much-admired illustrator of plant life.

Beatrix's grandfather, Edmund Potter, came from a Manchester family. His own grandfather was a flax merchant who was born in 1710. While his father, James Potter, was a merchant, Edmund became a printer and worked with his cousin, Charles, in this business. In

1825, he moved his wife and family to Dinting Lodge in Glossop. His partnership with his brother broke down in 1831 and Charles became a printer of wallpaper.

Edmund worked on his own and eventually, after many difficult times, introduced precision machine printing for calico which had previously been carried out by hand. By 1833, his mill employed three hundred and fifty workers, and had printed one million pieces of calico on forty two machines. Dinting Vale Printworks became the world's largest calico printing factory.

Edmund had seven children with his wife, Jessica Crompton, from Lancaster. Their son, Edmund, followed into his father's business in 1862 and their son, Rupert, became a barrister. Rupert, who lived to be 82, was the father of Beatrix Potter and her brother, Walter, who also became a respected artist.

Beatrix's grandfather, Edmund, was the Liberal Member of Parliament for Carlisle from 1861 until 1874. After being elected to Parliament, he spent more and more of his time living in London. He passed the overseeing of Dinting Vale to his son, Edmund. On retiring from parliament, he moved to Camfield Place, an estate which he had purchased in 1866. He died there on 26th October 1883.

His granddaughter would spend her summer holidays at Camfield and wrote 'The Tale of Peter Rabbit' there. She was also a very talented artist and made many drawings of the plant life on the estate.

In recent years the property was owned by Barbara Cartland and is still owned by her family. Barbara, the world-famous romantic novelist, wrote seven hundred and twenty four books and sold a billion copies making her the best-selling author in the world (Guiness Book of Records). She died at Camfield in 2000. She was buried next to an old Oak tree, said to have been planted in 1550 by Princess Elizabeth, who was living in Hatfield House at that time.

The Ebbs Family – Northaw & Ridge

Harry was the great grandson of Joseph Ebbs of Ridge in Hertfordshire, a village situated between South Mimms and Shenley, so named because of its elevated position in the countryside.

Harry's grandfather, James, was one of several brothers, the sons of Joseph, who were born in Ridge and who settled in the South Mimms area of Hertfordshire.

In 1815, the village, part of the manor of Shenley, comprised 3520 acres and had a population of 347. By 1871 this number had increased to 448. The village was about three miles in length and three quarters of a mile in width.

The village church, St Margaret's, is a 15th century building, having a tile covered chancel and nave, with a tower at the west end and a small porch. There are records of the Ebbs family being baptised, married and buried there throughout the years, often returning to the village from some considerable distance for these main events.

Harry's great grandfather, Joseph, worked as the bailiff of Tyttenhanger Farm, close to London Colney. His wife, Ann, died in 1814 and he married again. It is thought that he married Ann's sister, Sophia Smith, in the same year. Later Joseph became a local innkeeper.

The second son of Joseph and Ann, James Ebbs, was born in 1810. He worked as an agricultural labourer and lived in Ridge. He married Sarah who came from Stoke Newington in London.

They had twelve children. Sarah died at the age of 64 and James lived to be 81. Both were buried in the village in St Margaret's churchyard.

Their second son, Joseph, was born in 1843. He, like his father, was a labourer.

He and his wife, Harriet, born in Warwickshire, had eight children. Their eldest son, also Joseph, was born in 1866. He had three brothers, Charles, Henry (Harry) and William, as well as four sisters.

Joseph married Rosa who was born in Potters Bar, the marriage taking place in 1891. Joseph worked as a gardener, first living with his family in Darkes Lane, Potters Bar and then nearby in Cotton Road, off the High Street. He obtained work as a gardener at Mymmwood House in Shepherds Hill, a turning off the main road running from Potters Bar to Hatfield. Shepherds Hill makes a connection from there to The Ridgeway and Well Road, Northaw.

Joseph and his family lived in the Lodge while he was working on the estate of Mymwood House, the home of Archibald Thompson, a wealthy merchant and JP, who employed more than a dozen servants.

His large house was built about 1820 and had white rendered brickwork with a slate roof. It was used as a school and a care home for the elderly in later times. It is now being re-developed, following a valuation of about £2,000,000.

Joseph and Rosa had two sons, while they were living in the lodge, William Joseph, born in 1893, and Henry George, born in 1895.

The 1911 Census records their son, Henry, working as an under game-keeper at Hatching Green, Harpenden while his older brother, William Joseph, was still with his parents at the lodge and was also a gardener. At this time Joseph and Rosa had been married for twenty years.

Joseph's brother, Charles, born in 1870, became a bricklayer. When he was 22, he married Jane who was born in Axminster, Devon. She was five years older than Charles. They had four daughters and three sons and lived in Kensal Green and Willesden in North West London, and later in Tottenham and Edmonton in North London.

Joseph's brother, Henry (Harry) Ebbs was born when the family was living in Darkes Lane in 1878.

At an early age, Harry enlisted as a member of the 1st Battalion of the Welsh Regiment and served with it for eight years.

He was working at 'Northaw House' as a gardener when he married Ellen Goodrich in Barnet Register Office on 26th June 1910. Their son, Thomas Henry, was born on 19th September of that year at Bentley Heath between Potters Bar and Barnet, and then the family moved to Laurel Villa in Southgate Road, Potters Bar, a short distance away.

When Harry joined the army again in 1915, he was 38 and was still working and living in the lodge of 'Northaw House'.

He joined the 52nd Battalion of the Bedfordshire Regiment.

Records show that he was 5 feet and 6 inches tall and weighed 161 pounds. He served for four years, of which fifteen months were spent as a 'bomber' in France. On being demobbed, he had been promoted to the rank of sergeant.

He returned to his work as a gardener at Northaw at the age of 41 and remained there for another 20 years.

His younger, brother, William Joseph, born in Little Heath in 1885, served in the Royal Fusiliers (City of London Regiment) and was killed in action in 1916. His name is carved on the War Memorial on Northaw Village Green, together with another member of the Ebbs family, thought to be (William) Joseph, the son of Harry's older brother, Joseph, and who like Harry served in the Bedfordshire Regiment.

There is one important connection that the Ebbs Family makes.

The 1881 Census records Henry Ebbs, aged 32, a garden labourer, born at Ridge in Hertfordshire. With him was his wife, Sarah Ann, two years older and born in Staffordshire. He was Harry's uncle, the younger brother of Harry's father, Joseph.

What is remarkable is the fact that he was living in High Canons Lodge, only a short distance from Ridge, and was working for the Durant family!

Censuses show Henry and his wife, Sarah Ann, living in a cottage in New Road, Shenley, a short distance from High Canons. For how long Henry worked on the estate is unknown. At the age of 62, he was still recorded as a gardener.

The two mansions, 'Northaw House' and High Canons were linked. This time it was not by members of the wealthy Hertfordshire society!

4

'The Hook House' – Northaw

Opposite the Kidston Institute in Northaw Road is Hook Lane which runs south to Coopers Lane Road. It was in this lane that a poor house was opened by the parish council in 1783. Six years later it became a workhouse and housed about twelve people. The building was converted into cottages and some of the poor from Hatfield were moved there. The cottages were sold in 1862 to Nathaniel Brindley Acworth who owned 'The Hook', a large Victorian building which stood further south in Hook Lane, close to Coopers Lane Road.

The present house, an asymmetrical Tuscan-style villa, with white-painted stucco walls and a slate roof, was built in 1839 and incorporated an early 18th Century staircase. This was said to have come from 'Gobions House' in Brookmans Park when the property was demolished about this time. The house was built for Benjamin Cherry, a farmer of 103 acres.

The Cherry Family remained in 'The Hook' until the end of the 1850's when the Hertfordshire records (Kelly's Directories) show that the property was in the possession of Mr Nathaniel Brindley Acworth who remained there for over thirty years. The house would have been used, like several others in Northaw, as a 'country estate' as Mr Acworth does not appear on any census, in residence at the house, until 1891.

In 1861, Mr Charles Newton, 46, a retired general merchant, was living at 'The Hook'. He came from Hexham in Northumberland and his wife, Jane, aged 39, was born in Dublin, Ireland. They had a son and three daughters, all born in Sydney, New South Wales, Australia and under 15 years old. They employed a butler, a footman, a groom and four domestic servants who all lived in the house. A coachman and his wife were living in 'Hook Lodge', probably the Gate Lodge.

At this time the Hook Cottages, formerly the workhouse, were occupied by a cowman and two agricultural labourers with their families. They may have been working on the adjoining Hook Farm.

Charles Newton moved to Parham Park House in Sussex where he was recorded on the 1881 census. He was 66 and his wife, Jane, was 58. With them were their three daughters. Among their visitors was William B Sandeman, a brewer who was born in India, and Robert Sandeman, born in Perth, Scotland, a Lt Colonel with a Star of India. They had twelve servants living in the premises.

As stated above, in 1891 Mr Acworth was recorded at 'The Hook'. He was born in Rochester in Kent and was a JP for Hertfordshire and Middlesex.

Living with him at this time was his wife, Anne, who was born in Staffordshire. They employed a nurse, a butler, a footman, a cook and three maidservants. The gardener, who was also a domestic servant, lived with his wife and two very young daughters in the 'Gate Lodge', thought to be an even older, but very much smaller, building than 'The Hook' and situated on the corner of the lane and Coopers Lane Road.

'The Hook' was bought by George Roddick, a merchant engineer, in 1906. He was also a JP and lived there for more than twenty years. The 1911 census recorded George with his wife, Mary, from Annan in Dumfrieshire, having been married for 21 years. Their son, Charles, a project engineer, aged 20, was born in Calcutta, India. They employed a staff of six, female, general domestic servants living in the house.

Hertfordshire Records show that the Roddick family remained at 'The Hook' until it was sold to the Greyhound Racing Association in 1931. Following this purchase, the Association built a large number of kennels and appropriate buildings to develop their dog training programme over a period of nearly fifty years. The dogs would be transported from Northaw to racing stadia such as Haringay, Wembley and Walthamstow. Their trainers lived in the cottages in Hook Lane that had been occupied by labourers in earlier times.

In 1980 the whole estate of some 80 acres was sold to the Oshwal Association for £450,000. 'The Hook' has become 'Oshwal House' and a temple has been built in the grounds. The centre has now been used for over thirty years by the Jain community to propagate Jainism and its values through art, culture and education. The fundamental principles of Jainism are based on compassion and non-violence towards all living beings. Events are held in the Oshwal Centre when invited members from the Hindu, Sikh, Muslim, Jewish, Christian and Zoroastrian faiths take part in attempting to promote an understanding and friendship between people of different faiths and belief backgrounds through art, devotional songs and music.

And so, 'The Hook House' in Northaw, now the Oshwal centre, has been linked through the Cherry family to the Trotter Family of Dyrham Park and to the Durant Family.

The Cherry Family – Northaw and Brickendon

Land was purchased in Brickendon in 1805 by Benjamin Cherry, a butcher of Amwell in Hertfordshire and the grandfather, of Benjamin who built Brickendon Grange in 1859.

Before 1805 the Cherry family owned land around Brickendon Green. Benjamin's brother, John Cherry, inherited land, now known as Bentley's farm, when Benjamin died in 1817.

Before building Brickendon Grange, Benjamin Cherry, the butcher's grandson, built 'The Hook House' in Northaw. He lived there for some 19 years before moving to the Grange.

Benjamin was born in March 1809, the son of John Cherry, who was the son of Benjamin, the butcher of Amwell. He was admitted to Clare College, Cambridge at the age of 18 and obtained a Master's Degree in 1835 when he was 26. Two years later, he married Charlotte Cassandra, the daughter of Henry Phillpotts.

Much has been written about Henry Phillpotts, a man of extraordinary ability who had an outstanding career in the Church of England. Henry was born in May, 1778, in Bridgwater, Somerset, one of the 23 children of John Phillpotts, a factory owner, innkeeper, auctioneer and land agent of the Dean and Chapter of Gloucester Cathedral.

Jack Joel and the Prince of Wales

The Well at Childwick Green

St Mary's Church at Childwick Green

Kubrick Mannequin

Kubrick Mannequin

Otway House, Paignton

Kingshurst, now Kingsmount, Paignton

Brickendon Grange

Henry was educated at the Cathedral School before being admitted to Corpus Christi College, Cambridge at the age of 13. He received his BA there before taking a Master's Degree at Magdalen College by the age of 18. He took Holy Orders in 1802 when he was 24 and was ordained two years later.

He married Deborah Surtees in October 1804. She became the mother of his eighteen children, while he advanced his career in Durham and Chester before being consecrated as Bishop of Exeter in 1831.

It is impossible to summarise his career in the context of this work but it is sufficient to say that his contribution to the church is well-documented and easily accessible. He became known as 'Henry of Exeter', the longest serving bishop, in office from 1831 until 1869.

He did not find the accommodation near Exeter cathedral to his liking and, in 1841, had a palace built in Torquay to serve as his residence. 'Bishopstowe', now The Palace Hotel in Babbacombe Road, reminds one of this remarkable, 'fierce, fiery and intolerant' man.

He was buried in the churchyard of St Marychurch close by, in May 1778 at the age of 91. His wife Deborah, who died six years before him, was buried there as well. (see Kitson-Shiphay)

The church tower of St Marychurch was restored in his memory nearly a hundred years later. In addition, the Bishop Phillpotts Library in Truro, Cornwall was founded in 1856 and opened in 1871 for the use of the clergy in general.

In 1841 the census recorded Henry's daughter, Charlotte and Benjamin Cherry, her husband, living in 'The Hook' in Northaw together with their two young children, Marion, aged 2, and Benjamin Newman, newly born. Also living in the house were six servants.

Ten years later, the census records Benjamin as being 42 and Charlotte as 40. Marion was 12 but young Benjamin Newman Cherry was not with them. Three younger sons, Charles, aged 7, Henry, 6 , and Arthur, 2, were there. In addition five servants were living in the house. Benjamin was described as a landed proprietor, a fundholder and a farmer, as well as being a justice of the peace and a lieutenant of Hertfordshire.

By this time their young son had been sent away to a preparatory boarding school in Upper Richmond Road. The school run by a clergyman, Richard Trimmer, catered for about 40 boys with ages ranging from 9 to 15 years who came from as far as Scotland, Ireland, France and India. Four male teachers lived in the houses, two taught Classics, one taught French and one taught Mathematics. As well as Mr Trimmer, his wife, a son and two daughters, six servants lived in the premises.

In 1859, Benjamin left 'The Hook' in Northaw and arranged for the building of what was to be known as 'Brickendon Grange'. As stated, Benjamin's family already owned land in this area and he acquired more in the years that followed.

'Brickendon Grange', standing in forty acres of parkland and approached by a carriage driveway, had fourteen bedrooms and dressing rooms, three reception rooms, a schoolroom, a billiard room, a bathroom and entrance and inner halls. There was stabling for seven horses as well as fruit and vegetable gardens and glasshouses.

Benjamin and his wife Charlotte were recorded on the census of 1861, living in 'Brickendon Grange'. Young Benjamin Newman was with them and was an undergraduate of Clare College, Cambridge. Their children, Maria, aged 22; Charlotte, 17; Henry, 16; John, 9; and Madeleine, 7, were with them as well. A footman, a groom, a nurse, a cook and two maids were living in 'The Grange'. A gamekeeper and his family were living at Brickendon Green.

Benjamin Newman Cherry had been admitted to Clare College, Cambridge in 1857. He was awarded a BA Degree in 1862 and was a 'rowing blue' in 1860. He was ordained as a deacon in 1863 and became a priest in Worcester the following year. He moved to Northamptonshire where he held the curacy of Yardley Gobion. He married Rose Georgina Lennard from Western Australia on 23rd June 1868. Their son, Benjamin Lennard, was born in Yardley Gobion on 30th August 1869.

In 1871, Rose was living with her parents in-law at Brickendon, together with her son, Benjamin Lennard, aged 1. By this time, Rose's father-in-law had become a magistrate and his son, Benjamin, had just become the rector of Luddlington and Hemington. Benjamin and Rose had two more sons, Harold aged 6 and Herbert, 4, both born in Hemington and recorded on the 1881 census. Their brother, Benjamin, was not with them. He had been sent to boarding school at Winchester.

Benjamin Cherry, senior, died at the age of 65 in 1874 and his property, 'Brickendon Grange', passed to his eldest son, Benjamin Newman Cherry. He leased 'Brickendon Grange' to a Henry Demain Saunders. After Mr Saunder's death, the estate was sold to John Trotter, the son of John Trotter of Dyrham Park, who bought the freehold of the property from the Cherry family.

Benjamin Newman and his family moved to Clipsham, Rutland, in the diocese of Peterborough, where Benjamin was the rector from 1885 until 1905.

In 1891 Benjamin Lennard, then 21, was back with his family and was recorded as a student of law at Trinity College, Cambridge and the Inner Temple in London. Herbert, his younger brother, was a student at Winchester College at this time.

Benjamin Lennard became an LLB in 1891 having been admitted to the Inner Temple in the previous year. He moved to Lincoln's Inn in 1893 when he was 'called to the Bar'.

He married Laura Mary in 1896 and they had three daughters, Sylvia, Phoebe and Lydia, before their son, John, was born in 1906. The family was recorded on the 1911 census living at Harmer Green in Welwyn, Hertfordshire. Benjamin was recorded as a barrister.

Benjamin Lennard Cherry was a conveyancing counsel to the Supreme Court and a parliamentary draftsman. He was knighted in 1922 and he died on 13th September, 1932.

Another link was formed between two Hertfordshire families, the Cherry family and the Trotter family, when the freehold of 'Brickendon Grange' was purchased by John Trotter from Benjamin Newman Cherry.

5

'Northaw Place'

This was another large house which played an important part in the history of Northaw.

Kelly's Directory for 1937 describes the house – 'originally a Jacobean mansion and said to have been built by James I as a shooting-box, stands in a small park with an avenue of limes: the house has been added to extensively and contains mural paintings by Thornhill.'

In 1760 it was owned by Admiral Sir Richard Bickerton. It later came to John Pope and Thomas Blackford, members of the Goldsmiths Company. In 1800 it was owned by Thomas Gould. The 1841 Census records Ann Cameron , 45, living there, together with six servants.

From 1859 until 1862, Edward Lloyd Morgan was recorded as the owner. He was shown on the 1861 Census, aged 53, and a Stockbroker, born in Watling Street, Middlesex. With him were his wife, Katherine, 52, and four daughters and two sons, all born in Muswell Hill, London. He employed a cook and five maids. A gardener and a cowman, with their families, lived in the Lodge.

From 1870 until 1874 the house was occupied by John Mounsey. John Milner, 27, the gardener, born in Bolton, and his family lived in the Lodge. Mr Mounsey died at Sevenoaks in Kent in December 1887.

In 1881 The Census recorded a Mrs Agnes Troughton as being in residence. She was aged 51 and a widow who was born in Clun, Shropshire. She employed a cook, three maids, a footman and a groom. Thomas Williams, 32, the coachman, his wife Mary and young daughter, Catherine, were also recorded. At this time, John Milner and his wife were still living in the Lodge, when they had five sons and two daughters.

The 1891 Census recorded a gardener, William Dodson, 28, and his family in the house.

The house was acquired by the Reverend Frederic John Hall MA shortly after this and the property was converted into a preparatory school for boys. It was enlarged from its two storeys with hipped gable, flat roof and cupola, to its present three storeys. Numerous buildings were also added.

The 1901 Census records thirty four pupils in the school. There were also two assistant teachers, a German governess, eleven domestic staff and a groom.

In 1914 Charles Reynolds BA, R H Routledge MA and H B Nares White were living in "Northaw Place' Lodge' while Reverend Percy Cyril Underhill BA and Cecil Esdaile Winter MA were living in the house itself.

Kelly's Directory for 1922 showed Cecil Esdaile Winter MA at 'Northaw Place' and also at "Northaw Place' Preparatory School'. He was also recorded in the same capacity in 1929 (clearly the entry being out of date) Formerly the Reverend Hall's assistant, he was then in charge of the school, following Hall's retirement.

The school closed in 1928 and was bought as a private residence by Sir Philip Devitt who had been living at 'Foxholes' in Hitchin.

The Directory for 1933 records Sir Philip H Devitt Bart. at 'Northaw Place' and, again, in 1937 when John Marker was shown as his gardener.

In May 1935 children from the Parish, including John Holmes and Peter West, were invited to celebrate the Silver Jubilee of King George V at 'Northaw Place' with Sir Philip and Lady Devitt. All of the children were given mugs and spoons to commemorate the occasion.

Sir Philip still owned 'Northaw Place' in 1937 when he was 61, but in 1939 he moved to Pangbourne in Hertfordshire.

'Northaw Place' was leased to Middlesex County Council for a period before it was purchased by that council in 1965. It was used by the London Borough of Haringey as a Children's Home and in the 1970s the property was left empty.

In 1985 a number of very desirable dwellings were erected in the area that was formerly the stable block and courtyard.

Today, the new buildings provide first class accommodation but the house itself and some of its surroundings have fallen into a very poor structural and decorative state.

Much of the research in the following chapters relates to the Hall and Devitt families to illustrate how the history of 'Northaw Place' came about and how it was connected to so many other places in the country.

6

The Ancestors of Frederic Hall

Thomas Hall, the grandfather of Frederic Hall, and Thomas Clarkson – Wisbech

The Hall Family came to Northaw where they lived in 'Northaw Place', St Just, St Erth and Northacre. The following work illustrates how this happened and how other connections were made with Hertfordshire, Devon and Cornwall.

Two men were born in Wisbech, Cambridgeshire. Their birthdays were but seven years apart. Both were named Thomas and both their lives were to have very different effects upon the people of Hertfordshire.

Any visitor to the centre of Wisbech today could not help but notice a towering statue. It was designed by Sir George Gilbert Scott in 1880 and it overlooks the bridge spanning the River Neme. It was erected to commemorate probably the most notable person to be born in the town. He was Thomas Clarkson who was born in 1760.

Clarkson began his education in Wisbech at the Grammar School where his father, The Reverend John Clarkson, was the headmaster. At first, the school had been held in a room in St Peter's Church but later moved to a large house at the back of the Market Square in Hill Street. The school was in this building from 1549 to 1898. It is now the Conservative Club and the grammar school has moved to a much larger building 'over the bridge'.

From the grammar school, Clarkson moved to St Paul's School in London for a period of four years before going up to Cambridge, entering as a sizar to St John's College in 1779.

He obtained a scholarship the following year and in 1783 he became a deacon of the Church of England but never became a priest. He obtained his Masters Degree in 1786.

While at Cambridge he was awarded a prize for an essay he wrote in Latin that questioned the practice of slavery.

Shortly after this, on his way from Cambridge to London, he said that he made the decision to spend his life working towards the abolition of slavery. He wrote to William Wilberforce and discussed the issues with him. Wilberforce, a devout Christian, was a fellow student at St John's, as was a close friend, William Pitt, who was to become Prime Minister. Wilberforce, at first the MP for Hull, represented the views of those determined to abolish slavery in Parliament and fought their cause throughout his political career.

Clarkson travelled all over England, collecting evidence of slave trafficking and the cruelty of slavery, as well as enlisting public sympathy for his cause. He went to Paris in 1789 to gain the support of the French Government and visited the Czar in 1818.

His cause and his work are a part of British History.

During the 1790s he spent a good deal of his time writing, especially when he was a frequent guest of Joseph Hardcastle in his house in Hatcham, then a village in Surrey. Hardcastle was the First Treasurer of The Missionary Society. It was while there that Thomas met his future wife, Catherine Buck, a niece of Mrs Hardcastle.

By 1794 he was exhausted and retired from the campaign. He bought an estate in Ulleswater and became a close friend of William Wordsworth, the poet.

In 1796 he married Catherine, who was the daughter of William

Buck of Bury St Edmunds in Suffolk. William Buck was a wealthy yarn maker and a co-founder of the Greene King Brewery (see Lake Family).

While living in the Lake District, the Clarksons spent much of their time with the Wordsworths and Samuel Taylor Coleridge who were to become visitors when it was necessary for the Clarksons to return to Bury. There they lived in a large Georgian house in St Mary's Square for about ten years where their son, Thomas grew up.

Born in 1806, Thomas went to Rugby School and then to Cambridge before becoming a Barrister and the Magistrate of Thames Police Court.

In 1839 Clarkson was granted the Freedom of the City of London and lived latterly in Playford Hall, between Ipswich and Woodbridge, about 30 miles south west of Bury, where he became a gentleman farmer. He died there in September, 1846.

Another monument was erected in Hertfordshire in 1879 to commemorate the momentous decision that he made for his life's work. He is said to have stopped on the road at Wade's Mill and rested before taking refreshment in the Feathers Inn close by. While resting and thinking, his future was determined.

Thomas Hall, the grandfather of Frederic John Hall of 'Northaw Place', in Hertfordshire, was born in Croft, Lincolnshire in 1767. His family can be traced back to the 16th Century in the county and well into the 18th Century, long after he was born.

Thomas moved to Wisbech in Cambridgeshire, a busy market town and port at that time. There he started working as a draper. Of course, he had no idea what an influence his family was to have on the people of Hertfordshire .

When Thomas Hall was thirty five years old, long after Clarkson had left Wisbech, he married Mary Appleton Grainger on 5th January 1802 in Terrington, Yorkshire. Mary's family lived in Westow, close to York. She was fourteen years younger than Thomas.

Thomas and Mary built a thriving business in the town. They sold groceries as well as drapery and Thomas became a respected merchant.

He was deeply involved with St Peter's Church, where his children were baptised and attended services throughout their childhood.

By the time he retired from his work he had become quite wealthy and he and Mary lived in a delightful Georgian house in The Crescent, close to the church, in the old and picturesque part of the town. They were there until Thomas died in 1851 at the age of 84. Mary moved close by into Church Street, now known as Church Terrace. She was listed as a member of the Gentry in 1853 in the Norfolk County Directory.

Their children were born in Wisbech during the first seventeen years of their marriage. They had seven sons and two daughters before 1819.

Their second son, Grainger, born in 1806, died when he was 7. Two of their boys, William and Charles, followed into their father's drapery business. William became a tailor as well as a draper, living in Guyhim, an area close to Wisbech. While William married Jane and had four children, Charles remained unmarried at 36 and was living in The Crescent with his parents and his older unmarried sister, Mary Ann who was 39. Another son, Richard became a mariner in the Merchant Service in the thriving port that Wisbech was at this time. He married and had two children.

It was the sons of Thomas and Mary Hall, Thomas Grainger Hall and Henry Hall, who forged the links with Hertfordshire.

Thomas Grainger Hall, father of Frederic Hall, in London & Paignton

Thomas Grainger Hall, the eldest son of Thomas Hall and Mary Grainger, was born in 1803. He matriculated in 1820 and entered Magdalene College, Cambridge as a sizar, with reduced fees and having certain menial duties, at the age of seventeen. He took his BA with First Class Honours in Mathematics four years later, when he was made a Fellow of the College. He was also a tutor there for seven years, taking his Masters Degree in 1827 when he was ordained as a Deacon at Ely before becoming a Priest the following year.

After his teaching at Cambridge, he was made Professor of

Mathematics at Kings College in London where he remained until his retirement in 1869.

He was, undoubtedly, a brilliant mathematician who, during his career from 1840 to 1863, wrote several books relating to the study of Mathematics – Algebra, Geometry and Arithmetic. Perhaps his best known works were, and still are, 'An Elementary Treatise on the Differential and Integral Calculus' and 'A Treatise on Plane and Spherical Trigonometry'. Copies of these works are currently available.

While working at Kings, he had several addresses in London and clearly mixed in the London Society of this time. It was here that he met Eliza Kitson. He was to marry her in 1831.(see Kitson Family)

Eliza Kitson, was born in Ashburton in Devon in 1808. Many members of her immediate family who came from Exeter in Devon were working and living in London and had been students at Cambridge, while Thomas was a student and a tutor there. It is also probable that others attended Kings College, studying Mathematics. The Kitsons had addresses in the parish of Hanover Square in London and, no doubt, Eliza was a part of the society in which Thomas mixed, particularly during the London 'Season', and attended the church that he attended.

Eliza and Thomas were married in Paignton, Devon on 28th December 1831. Their eldest child, a daughter, Georgina, was born a year later but died on 6th August 1841. Her short life was recorded on a Monumental Inscription, with that of her parents, in Coverdale Church Yard in Paignton.

Thomas and Eliza had four sons and three more daughters but only three of their sons survived. Their daughters, Mary Ann and Emily Georgina were born in Pimlico in St Peter's Parish.

The censuses for 1841 and 1851 show Thomas and his family living in Chester Square in the Parish of St George's, Hanover Square where their son, George Thomas, was baptised as was their youngest son, Edward Grainger Hall, who was born in 1849.

Although their son, Frederic John's, birth took place in a large house in the Tormoham area of Torquay in 1847, the family was still living in London.

The house where Frederic was born was called 'Wenlock' and was a large villa, built on the high ground outside of Torquay, overlooking the sea and the harbour. It was one of many built by William Kitson (see Kitson Family), and was, no doubt, being used as a summer residence by the Hall family. Later 'Wenlock' was occupied by Baroness Louisa Aylmer for a period before its name was changed. It remains largely in its original state today. It is now known as 'Merton Lodge' and is in Middle Lincombe Road at the junction with Ridgeway Road.

Ten years later, the family were living at 'Elms Leigh' in Wandsworth, 'south of the river'. It was while they were living in this area that they became the close friends of the Attlee family who lived in Portinscale Road. Henry Attlee was a Solicitor of the Supreme Court of Justice and, in 1881, when he was 39, he and his wife Ellen had six children. Their son Clement, who was to become Prime Minister, had not been born at this time. Their friendship with the Halls came through their attendance at the same church.

At this time, Thomas was a Prebendary of St Paul's Cathedral as well as undertaking his teaching post at Kings. He and Eliza sent their three sons to Shrewsbury School in Shropshire where they all had successful careers.

Thomas retired from his teaching post at Kings and he and his wife, Eliza, and their son, Edward, a student of London University, returned to Eliza's 'home town' of Paignton on the shores of Tor Bay.

At the beginning of the 19th Century, Paignton was described as 'a neat and improving village and bathing place'. Much of that old village remains around the village church of St John the Baptist. While, in 1801, the population of Paignton was shown as 1575, by 1851 it had risen to 2746 and in 1901 it was 8385. Clearly the population trebled in the last half of that century, largely due to the popularity of the bathing and the fact that the railway reached the town in 1859, on a direct route from London to Torquay, making it an ideal holiday resort.

When the Halls moved to their mansion, 'Kingshurst', in 1869 most of the development in Paignton was centred close to the sea front. Their very large Victorian building stood in splendid isolation towards the back of the town, about half a mile to the north west of the Parish Church. It stood on high ground with sea views and was situated in spacious grounds and approached by a long carriageway. It was five years after this that another property was built in the area.

Today the house is used as a Nursing Home for Elderly People and has had some extensions made for this purpose. Sadly, perhaps, the views that once were a delight no longer exist, as surrounding building in recent years has completely changed the environment.

The nearest property to 'Kingshurst' was 'Oldway' the home of Isaac Singer and his family. This was a huge mansion having one hundred and fifteen rooms. The American millionaire who made a fortune from the development and sale of sewing machines arrived in Devon in 1870 before settling in Paignton, in the house built for him in 1874. Much has been written about Isaac Singer's life and that of his descendents and it is of interest to note that he was not accepted by the 'gentry' of that time as he had become rich through his commercial enterprise.

It is evident that Thomas Hall was well acquainted with the family. He makes provision in his Will that a copy of the Works of Shakespeare, presented to him by Mrs Singer, be left to his son Edward. There is no doubt that the Singer family contributed a huge amount to the development of Paignton in many ways before they left in 1914. Today 'Oldway' has been acquired by the Torbay Council.

The Halls certainly were accepted into the 'society' of Paignton, in spite of Thomas's father being a draper in Wisbech! Obviously his education and his involvement with the Church of England counted for everything and illustrated the power behind the church at this time.

Although Thomas had retired from his active life at King's College in London, he remained as a Prebendary of St Paul's Cathedral and surely worked with Frederick Poland, the vicar, of St John's, Paignton. Certainly, the families were closely associated through the Parish Church.

Both Thomas and Eliza remained at 'Kingshurst' until they died,

Thomas in 1881, at the age of 78, and Eliza in 1899 when she was 90. The East Window of the Parish Church has a dedication to them. Similarly there is a dedication to Reverend Frederick W Poland, who was the vicar until 1891, and his daughters, Maud and Mary who died in 1889 and 1891.

On his death, Thomas's estate was assessed as being almost £24,000. On the death of Eliza, £5000 was given to each of his daughters and the remainder divided between the three sons.

In 1901 Emily Hall, Thomas' daughter, was still living in Paignton in a house called 'Treganna'. She was unmarried, aged 59, and was employing a cook and a housemaid. In 1910 she was living in 'South Mount' in Southfield Road.

Henry Hall, brother of Thomas G Hall – St Alban's Abbey and School

Henry was the ninth and youngest child of Thomas Hall and Mary Appleton Grainger of Wisbech in Cambridgeshire. He was baptised in St Peter's Church in August 1819.

It might have been expected that he would follow in his older brother, Thomas's, footsteps to the Grammar School in Wisbech. However, this was not the case.

Henry was more than sixteen years younger than Thomas and, by the time he was ready for a formal education, his brother was a tutor in King's College, London. Clearly it was felt that this was a better option for the boy and Henry entered the college, gaining his Matriculation in 1837.

At the age of seventeen, he was admitted sizar, with reduced fees and having certain menial duties, to Magdalene College, Cambridge, Again, he followed his brother, studying Theology and Mathematics.

In 1841, he took a Bachelor of Arts Degree with First Class Honours in Mathematics and became a Fellow of the College at this time. He was ordained Deacon the following year when he became the domestic chaplain to Lord Monson, a role which he retained for eighteen years.

He received a Master of Arts Degree in 1844 and became a priest the year after. He was appointed by the trustees as the new Headmaster of St Albans Grammar School in Hertfordshire in the same year.

St Alban's School was founded in 948 by Abbot Wulsin and is the oldest school in Hertfordshire, as well as being one of the oldest in the United Kingdom. In the beginning, the education of the pupils took place in the abbey church and, by 1100, the school had built a high reputation for itself. The school remained under the control of the Abbot until the dissolution of the Abbey in 1539.

In 1549 the last Abbot was granted the right to establish a Grammar School by a private Act of Parliament. In 1553 the Abbey Church was sold to the town for £400 and became a Protestant Parish Church for the new Borough of St Albans.

The Lady Chapel of the Abbey was walled off from the main body and a public passageway was created from north to south. In this separated chapel the Grammar School was situated for the next three hundred years. It was not until 1871, when the school was transferred to the great gateway, that the Lady Chapel was reunited with the main body of the church.

It was to this Lady Chapel that Henry Hall was appointed, as Head Master of St Albans Grammar School, in 1845. It was here that he would spend the next 18 years of his life.

He faced an uphill task as the school had deteriorated considerably in more recent times under the leadership of his predecessor, who was obliged to retire from his position as headmaster, there being no more than a dozen scholars present at any one time.

At first he met with considerable difficulties. There was obviously great animosity between the under master, who had been appointed at the same time, and Henry. Their differences appear to have stemmed from their beliefs in whether or not pupils should receive a classical or commercial education, according to their needs.

In any event there was little response from the local population in sending their sons to the school. Most only saw the need for young boys to be working, assisting in running their businesses or trades, or working for others, rather than spending their time learning through an education at school.

Hall had to attempt to cater within one school, with limited space, for the needs of both 'day boys' and 'boarders'. A majority of the former were the sons of local traders, some perhaps less affluent and not so ambitious for their sons' levels of attainment and who may have required a less formal education, particularly in the Classics, whereas the boarders, drawn from affluent backgrounds, were, no doubt, seeking University places.

It should be remembered that Hall was the son of a merchant of Wisbech. His father was nevertheless a man of some standing and certainly wanted the best for his sons. Two of them became distinguished classical scholars. It may have been Henry's background that led him to desire to maintain classical standards of education in his school for all of those in his care.

Henry married Elizabeth Stevens from Wisbech in the summer of 1849 and he and his wife lived in Fishpool Street, a very short distance from the abbey in St Albans. The 1851 Census recorded them with twenty nine 'boarders', a cook and three domestic servants. Of the twenty nine boarders, thirteen were from Cambridgeshire and four from Wisbech, the home town of Henry and Elizabeth.

The school prospered under his leadership and considerable progress was made by his pupils. Reports by inspectors on the achievement of the pupils in the Classics, History and Geography were glowing, as was that of the inspector of Mathematics. The report on Religious Education stated that their achievement reflected much credit on themselves and the system of education pursued in the school.

In the later years of his leadership, he employed six 'ushers' (temporary and part-time assistant teachers) to give instruction in Drawing, Writing, French, German, Drilling and Music to meet the demands of an ever-widening curriculum.

The 1861 census recorded the fact that Henry and Elizabeth had moved to Laburnum Street, again close to the school. However, at this time, there were only five pupils 'boarding' with them, and only one was from Wisbech! Henry's three children were with them, as were five servants.

This is a clear indication that the number of pupils at the school who were boarders had considerably reduced and, as there were approximately nine or ten times that number on roll at the school, most pupils were coming from the town on a daily basis.

Perhaps Henry became disillusioned after his eighteen years at St Albans or felt the need for a change. No doubt his salary had lessened, as he was obliged to pay for the ushers himself from the salary he received, and he was unable to achieve the level of scholarship to which he aspired. However he had achieved a great deal in his time there and his results had been duly noted by all of those connected with the school.

In 1863, he and his family left Hertfordshire and returned to his native Cambridgeshire where he had been educated. He became the Vicar of St Paul's Church in the City itself. He, Elizabeth and their children, lived in Parsonage House, attached to St Paul's Church. They were recorded, living at this address, on the 1871 Census.

Their eldest daughter, Mary Grainger Hall, married John Edwin Sandys in 1880. John, the son of a clergyman working for the Church Missionary Society in India, was educated at Repton School and St John's College Cambridge where he became a Fellow and worked as a tutor and lecturer in Classical Studies. He was elected as Public Orator in 1876 and received doctorates at several British Universities as well as in Greece. He was made a Fellow of the British Academy in 1909 and was awarded a knighthood in 1911. He and Mary had no children and John died in Cambridge at the age of 78.

Henry's daughter, Sarah Elizabeth, became a scholar and taught Classics for most of her life. She remained unmarried and in her later years lived in a flat in a fashionable part of Bayswater, London.

Their son, Reginald, returned to Hertfordshire, being sent to Haileybury College, in Great Amwell, where his uncle, Frederic John Hall was a master. He matriculated in 1879 and was admitted to St

The Clarkson Memorial in Wisbech

The Old Grammar School in Wisbech

The Crescent, Wisbech

THE
OLD GRAMMAR
SCHOOL
1549–1898
HERE ALSO THE BURGESSES
HELD THEIR MEETINGS FOR TWO
HUNDRED AND FIFTY YEARS:
AND HERE WAS BORN IN 1760
THOMAS CLARKSON
"FRIEND OF THE
SLAVES"

Clarkson Memorial Plaque

Clarkson Memorial – Wadesmill in Hertfordshire

St Blaise Church, Haacombe in Devon

TORBAY CIVIC SOCIETY

THE
HOME AND OFFICES OF

WILLIAM KITSON
1800 – 1883

SOLICITOR, LAND AGENT,
LOCAL AUTHORITY CHAIRMAN,
BANKER AND CHURCHWARDEN

THE MAKER OF
TORQUAY

Kitson Plaque in Vaughan Parade, Torquay

Restoration of Shiphay House, outside of Torquay

Sharpham House, Devon

Trelawne House in Cornwall

Cockington Manor, Torquay

Grave of Richard Durant in Ashprington

John's College Cambridge, where his brother-in-law was a Fellow. He passed, as a University Candidate, into the RMC Sandhurst in 1881 and became a lieutenant in the Royal Warwickshire Regiment. He was made a captain seven years later. He went to South Africa as a War Correspondent in 1899 and joined the South African Light Horse. His death occurred in May 1914.

Elizabeth died in December 1875 but Henry remained in the Parsonage until he retired in 1890. In his later years, he lived at 15 Brookside in Cambridge where he died at the age of 77.

7
Family Connections of Thomas G Hall

When Thomas Grainger Hall married Eliza Kitson, he became a part of one of the most influential families in the South West of England.

The Kitson Family – Ashprington in Devon

Thomas, born in 1485, the son of Robert Kitson (Kytson), came from the village of Yealand (Yelland) in the Parish of Warton in Lancashire. As a young man he travelled to London where he became an apprentice of Richard Glasyer, a mercer and merchant adventurer. He became free of the City in 1507 and was trading on his own account in a substantial manner two years later, dealing with the broadcloths of Hampshire, Wiltshire and Somerset.

He became one of England's wealthiest merchants of the time, not only dealing with cloth but also trading in satins, laces, cloth of gold, velvets, furs and tapestries. Much of his merchandise came from Flanders where he had a fine house and many servants.

His rising prosperity allowed him to purchase extensive areas of land and properties in Suffolk, Devon, Dorset, Somerset and Nottinghamshire. He mixed with nobility and became a close friend of the Duke of Buckingham from whom he purchased the manor of Hengrave in Suffolk. Here he built 'Hengrave Hall', which took about thirteen years to complete. Hengrave was established as his family home. In addition to this he retained a London house in Milk Street, off Cheapside, and a suburban residence in Stoke Newington.

He served as a sheriff of London in 1533 and was knighted in the same year. He was also a warden and master of the Mercers' Company and remained a member of the Merchant Adventurers' Club until his death at Hengrave in 1540.

Thomas and his second wife, Margaret Donnington, had four daughters and a son, also named Thomas, born after his father had died. This son married twice but provided no male heir to the Hengrave estate which passed down the female side of the family. Margaret married twice after Thomas's death, her third husband being the Earl of Bath.

It would appear that Thomas must have ensured that members of the Kitson family had claims to some of his lands before he died, or that his wife, who inherited his property after his death, passed some of it to members of his family.

Any records between the time of Thomas's death and a time nearly two hundred years later provide little help in illustrating how events took place but records do show that many members of the Kitson family were to be found throughout the British Isles during the 17th and 18th Centuries, not least in Devon and Cornwall where the family was both prosperous and influential.

More than one hundred years after the death of Thomas Kitson, a William Kitson was born on 22nd January 1659 in the parish of Warton in Lancashire, where Thomas, together with many other members of the Kitson family, was born.

There is no evidence to be sure that this William Kitson was he who was to be found in Devon 37 years later but it could be so and prove to be the link between the Kitsons of Lancashire and Devon.

William Kitson occupied the property known as Painsford Manor, situated between Ashprington and Harbertonford, reasonably close and south of Totnes in Devon. The property, a 17th Century house in the valley of the River Harbourne, was owned by the Kellond family for whom William worked as an agent, as well as carrying out a form of private banking.

It is impossible to gain any idea of what the original manor house was like by viewing the existing building which is now a farmhouse. It was probably built in the late 16th Century but was remodelled by John Kellond in the late 17th Century and altered again in the early 19th. It was undoubtedly much larger than the present building and had long wings and open loggias adjacent to the main building. Today, this building appears to be on different levels throughout and is probably the result of the alterations. The present façade has been rendered and painted white which has ruined the character of the house that is evidenced by the stone work at the rear and sides.

There was a chapel on the site in the 14th Century and, again, this was rebuilt by John Kellond but was no longer in use in the 18th Century.

The property had been purchased by John Kellond in 1647. He became Sheriff of Devon in 1666. His son went to America and it is probable that the property became vacant about the time of William Kitson's possible arrival in Devon.

In St David's Church in Ashprington there is a large, imposing memorial of Portland stone and marble, erected at the end of the 17th Century, to honour the lives of the Kellonds, who were, undoubtedly, a very prominent local family.

On 22nd April 1698, William Kitson and Mary Hill were granted a licence to marry. Both were shown in the Devon & Cornwall Licences list as being of Ashprington. However no record has been found of where their marriage took place.

William was recorded as a churchwarden in St David's Church in Ashprington for twenty five years from 1700 until 1725 and he and his family were obviously closely associated with the church, so much so that William and Mary's daughter, Mary, married the Rector, William Marshall. He was forty six and she was twenty and his third wife. He was a legendary figure who was said to have had massive strength, being able to lift huge weights. He is thought to have lifted three men sitting on a bench on to a table and, when a horse and cart blocked his way in a narrow lane, he threw them over a hedge! Hardly the behaviour of a rector, one would think.

He was the rector from 1706 until 1756 when he died, aged 80. William Marshall and Mary's son, Henry, died on Christmas Day in the year of his birth, 1725. William had lost two sons and a daughter in early childhood during his previous marriages. Mary lived for another 29 years and was buried with her husband in St David's Church.

William Kitson of Painsford's son, William, born two years before his sister, Mary, married on 6th July 1722. His wife, another Mary, was the daughter of Rawlin Mallock who owned Cockington Court, the Manor House in the picturesque village of Cockington, a mile from the Devon coast.

The Mallock Family were very rich silversmiths from Exeter who occupied the Manor from the middle of the 14th Century until 1927. Roger Mallock purchased the house in 1654 from the Cary family who had owned it for 279 years but who were obliged to sell it, having lost much of the family fortune during the Civil War. Roger's son, Rawlin, who became a JP and an MP made extensive alterations and additions to the house, introducing a walled garden and ponds, as well as enclosing the parkland. When he died in 1690 the property was held in trust by his wife, Elizabeth, until his son, Rawlin, succeeded to take the estate on reaching the age of 18 in 1699. However he died in 1700 and the estate passed to another Rawlin, the grandson of Richard Mallock who was also in the family business in Exeter. This Rawlin had eight daughters and a son, yet another Rawlin, born in 1708, who succeeded to the estate in 1750.

It was his eldest sister, Mary, born in 1701, who married William Kitson in 1722. This marriage surely illustrates the social status of the Kitson family at this time.

William Kitson and Mary Mallock's son, William, was born in 1723 and a year later another son, Rawlin, was born. A daughter, Mary, was born at the beginning of 1727 and another son, John, was born in the summer of 1728.

William lost his first wife, Mary (Mallock), and was recorded as marrying Ann Lear, the daughter of Thomas Lear of Sandwell Manor near Harberton in July 1735. Their sons, also born in Painsford, were Thomas, born in 1736, Henry in 1737 and Walter, in 1741, and were, therefore, half brothers to William, Rawlin and John.

In 1742 William and his family left Ashprington, having bought Shiphay Manor which was to become the family seat of the Kitsons.

Walter Kitson – a link with Northaw

It was through the family of William's youngest son, Walter, that another connection with Northaw in Hertfordshire was made.

Walter married Martha, the daughter of Edward Addicott on 25th June, 1771 in St Stephen's Church, Exeter. Their sons Edward and Walter both became clergymen following their education at Oriel College, Oxford.

Walter gained his Masters Degree in 1804 when he was the vicar of St Eval in Cornwall before moving to Somerset where he died at the age of 65.

Edward became the Vicar of St Marychurch, a village just outside of Babbacombe, in 1797 and remained there for thirty years. He and his wife, Margaret Blake, had three sons who, again, became clergymen.

Their son, Edward, followed in his grandfather's footsteps at Balliol where he gained his MA in 1827 before he became a Chaplain in the Royal Navy as well as working at Greenwich Hospital for twenty years. Later he moved back to Devon, becoming Rector of North Huish, a village just a short distance from Totnes. He stayed there for three years before his death in 1873.

While he was serving in the Royal Navy, his son, the great grandson of William of Ashprington, was born in Malta. He was Edwin Bredin Blake Kitson who was sent to Merchant Taylors School in London before going to Christ's College in Cambridge. He was ordained deacon in 1866 and gained an MA the following year. He became Chaplain to the Forces from 1868 to 1893 in Woolwich, Nova Scotia, Gosport, and Aldershot before becoming the Vicar of Northaw in Hertfordshire from October, 1893 until 30th June 1914 when he resigned. Of course he would have conducted the services there that were attended by the Hall family. He was also the Rural Dean of Barnet in Hertfordshire from 1909 until he retired from Northaw. He died in Putney in 1918.

Thomas Kitson – 'Shiphay' in Devon

William of Ashprington's eldest son, Thomas, was born in 1736 before the family moved to Shiphay. He married Henrietta Ley of Kingskerswell, a neighbouring village to Shiphay. The marriage took place in St Paul's Church, Exeter, on 9th February 1766.

Sadly, Henrietta died the following year, after the birth of twins, William and Robert. From 1763 until 1803 Thomas became the Vicar of Torre with Cockington and from 1803 until his death in 1815, he was the Vicar of Abottskerswell.

Thomas's son, William, one of the twins born in 1769, went up to Oriel College, obtaining his MA when he was 26. He married Susanna, the daughter of Robert Abraham of Garrington on 26th September 1797. The ceremony was conducted by his cousin, Edward.

He became the rector of North Lew, a Devon village north west of Okehampton and on the edge of Dartmoor. In 1803 he was appointed Vicar of Torre with Cockington, following in his father's footsteps. He became Vicar of Abbotskerswell, following his father again. He remained in that office until his death on 1st February 1847. He was recorded living at Shiphay House on the 1841 census, having inherited the manor in 1815. He was aged 70 and his wife, Susanna, was 60.

William and Susanna had four sons and three daughters between 1798 and 1814.

Their eldest son, Thomas, born in 1798, was educated at Crediton and Westminster before graduating at Baliol College, Oxford in 1819. He became the curate of the Reverend W.B.Wray at Coombe-in-Teignhead before taking on the curacy of Haccombe, a very small village 3 miles south east of Newton Abbot. The few houses nearby the church were dominated by Haccombe House, built on the site of an ancient hall at the beginning of the 19th Century. This was the seat of the Carew family.

The small church, now decorated with a pink finish, stands a short distance from the house which is now used as a nursing home. Thomas married Mary Luckem who came from nearby Shaldon on the estuary of the River Teign. Their first three daughters were born in Coombe-in-Teignhead before the family moved to Shiphay Manor when Thomas inherited the property from his father who died in 1847. Two more daughters were born there. The family was recorded on the 1871 Census at Shiphay where they employed a butler, a groom, a footboy, a needlewoman and two maids.

Thomas became a Justice of the Peace for Devon and was chaplain to the Newton Abbot Union. He was buried at St Marychurch, aged 82.

His wife, Mary, 75, and her three unmarried daughters, Henrietta, Frances and Anne, aged 50, 48 and 41, together with six servants, were still living at Shiphay in 1881, after Thomas's younger brother, William, had inherited the manor (see below). Mary died two years later.

William and Susanna's third son, Robert, born in 1801, graduated at Exeter College, Oxford, and gained his MA nine years after his older brother, Thomas. He became the vicar of Dean Prior, a village on the edge of Dartmoor, where he lived in the vicarage with his wife, Frances, and their three servants and a gardener.

William and Susanna's second son, William, born in 1800, the younger brother of Thomas, was educated at Chelston until he was 10, when he was sent to Blundell's School in Tiverton. Later he studied Law in the offices of his uncle, Robert Abraham, in Ashburton. Robert was the solicitor of the Palk Family, one-time wealthy landowners.

The Palks resided in the town of Ashburton when this was a flourishing and prosperous area of the clothing trade in the 18th Century. The Palk and Abraham families were farmers and were joined by marriage. Walter Palk, a yeoman farmer and carrier of cloth, married Frances Abraham, the daughter of a wealthy farmer living in the same district.

Their son, Robert Palk, who was born in 1717, was educated at Ashburton Grammar School before going up to Oxford. He was ordained and took a curacy in Cornwall. Unhappy in this role, he joined the Navy as a Chaplain and later carried on this work for the East India Company. He resigned his chaplaincy but still worked for the company. He was offered the role of Governor of Madras and travelled to India where he excelled in business on his own account and returned to Devon as a very rich man. He bought the Manors of Tormorhan, Torwood and Tor Key in 1768 when the area was largely rural. The Palks became the landowners of the major part of what became Victorian Torquay.

The Palk Family invested heavily in the development of the area and, when Sir Robert died in 1798, at the age of 81, his son, Lawrence, inherited his estate. He did not inherit his father's business acumen or his desire to work with grit and determination to succeed. He spent a good deal of money in the development of the harbour area of Torquay, believing that this would bring increased trade to the area, but was slow to recognise the potential of Tormoham and did not believe that any systematic development would be beneficial. He preferred to live the life of a country gentleman, engaged in rural pursuits. Lawrence's son had even less aptitude for financial affairs and was far more interested in spending his money on drinking, gambling and womanising. Slowly he fell heavily into debt and was obliged to flee from England to France. While in France, his family's affairs were in the hands of his agent, William Kitson.

Following his training with Robert Abraham, where he would have become familiar with the Palk family's affairs, as Robert was a steward of the family estates, William began practising as a solicitor in Torquay. He set up his practice in Vaughan Parade, Torquay.

In 1832 he married Georgiana, the daughter of John Lane Kitson and the twin sister of Eliza, born in Ashburton in 1810. They lived over the offices in the Parade. In the same year, William established the Torbay Bank with rooms in his law office in Vaughan Parade until it was moved to No. 1 Vaughan Parade. It remained there and was taken over by Lloyds Bank in 1900. When his uncle died in 1833, Kitson was put in charge of the Palk estates and he worked in professional law, banking and estate management. He maintained a tight control over the estates until 1874.

In that time he encouraged and guided the development and improvement of Torquay. He influenced all the building that took place on the Palk lands, ensuring that any work was of a quality in keeping with the development of a fashionable resort for the wealthy. On the hills around the harbour, the villas, mansions and large, palatial, homes with their superb sea views are still in evidence today as examples of Kitson's achievement.

As chairman of the Local Authority his contribution in the planning and supervision of residential housing estates and the development of a system of roads was inestimable. The claim that he 'made' Torquay was undisputed. At this time, he was one of the few male members of the Kitson family not to become a clergyman. Nevertheless, he became Chairman of the Torquay branch of the Church Association and was instrumental in the founding of two churches in the area.

William and Georgiana had a daughter, named after her mother, as well as four sons, William Henry, John, George and Robert who followed their father into working in the law offices and banking in Torquay.

In 1861, the census recorded William and Georgiana living in Vaughan Parade with their son William, a banker, John, an attorney at law and their daughter, Georgiana, then 21. They employed housemaids, a cook, a groom and a stable boy.

The family moved away from Vaughan Parade in 1865. The 1871

Census recorded William living in Edginswell, a village a short distance from Shiphay. His house was called 'Hengrave' and, surely, indicates the belief in the links between his family and the Kitsons of Hengrave in Suffolk. He was recorded as a banker, landowner, and farmer of 250 acres employing 8 men. As well as his wife, Georgiana, their son, Robert, then 28, who had become a Solicitor, was living with them. They employed a cook, two maids and a stable boy.

William lived at 'Hengrave' after he retired until his death in April 1883. He inherited Shiphay in 1880 but preferred to remain at 'Hengrave'. His son Robert, a banking assistant was still living with his mother and father in 1881 when he was 37. Georgiana lived until July 1896

His elder son, William Henry, born in 1833 became a banker, and married Edith Kennedy who was born in Shrewsbury, Shropshire.

They were living in a house known as 'Hemsworth' in Tormoham in 1881 when they employed three domestic servants and a gardener. William Henry inherited Shiphay on the death of his father, and was recorded as living there on the 1901 Census. There were six servants in residence. William Henry died in 1904 and Edith lived until 1922.

William Kitson's son and William Henry's brother, John, became a banker. In 1891 he was shown on the census as living at 'Fairfield' on the Teignmouth Road with his wife, Mary, who was born in Hornsey, Middlesex, and three servants. In 1901 John, then retired, with Mary and five servants was at 'Hengrave'. On his brother's death, in 1904, he inherited 'Shiphay' as William and Edith had no children.

Later, 'Shiphay' and 'Hengrave' passed to John's cousin, Charles William in 1911, and on his death to his brother, Robert Paul Kitson, in 1922. They were the sons of Charles Kitson, the third son of the Reverend William Kitson.

Charles, born in 1814, became a solicitor and worked with his older brother, William. At first he lived with him and his family in Vaughan Parade, Torquay. After his marriage he moved to 'Collaton' a large house in Old Torwood Road, Tormoham, and was recorded on the 1861 Census with his wife, Caroline, and their five children, including Charles William and Robert Paul. They employed two nurses, a cook, a maid, and a gardener.

Charles William followed his father in becoming a solicitor in the family business. At the age of 33, he was living with his wife, Melina, the daughter of a retired major in the Bengal Army, and their three children in the house of his widowed aunt, Mary Best. The house was 'Lisburn' on the Lower Warberry Road in Tormoham. The staff consisted of a housekeeper, a cook, four maids. a page, a valet and a gardener.

Robert Paul Kitson, who also worked in the family business inherited 'Collaton' and he was living there in 1901 with his wife, Adela, who was born in County Limerick, Ireland. She was seven years older than Robert and they had no children.

In 1922, Robert moved to 'Hengrave' and enlarged the property while letting 'Shiphay'.

At the end of the First World War, the members of the Board of Governors of Torquay Hospital believed that it was necessary to relocate the existing hospital and they took steps to find a site suitable to house a new, much enlarged and modern building. Discussions took place over a long period of time between the Board and the civic authorities. There were views for and against any proposals but eventually the building of a new hospital was agreed in principle.

A site for the building, thought to be suitable for what was needed, was offered by Robert Paul Kitson. He believed that 'Hengrave Hall', together with 15 acres of land, was ideal, at a greatly reduced price of £8,000. Many were in agreement but, again, there were arguments put forward against this proposal. At the end of the day, a Mrs Ella Rowcroft, a member of the Wills Tobacco family, became the saviour of those much in favour of this improvement. By her making a gift, to cover the cost of the purchase of 'Hengrave Hall', all former concerns quickly disappeared. The new hospital was built around the old house which, today, accommodates the offices of the Hospital Trust and remains a firm reminder of the Kitson family, at the centre of this massive development.

'Shiphay Manor' was also sold by Robert Paul Kitson in 1929. It was the subject of many changes in its appearance and its use in the following years. Recently it has undergone considerable renovation but remains a constant reminder of the days gone by as it is used by the staff and pupils of Torquay Grammar School.

Henry Kitson – Ashburton, Exeter and Crediton in Devon

When William Kitson married Georgiana on 24th September 1832 in Paignton Church the ceremony was conducted by his father, the Vicar of Abbotskerswell. They were following in the footsteps of Georgiana's twin sister, Eliza, who had married Thomas Grainger Hall in the same church, with a service conducted by the same vicar, a service that took place on 28th December 1831 nearly nine months before.

Georgiana and Eliza were the granddaughters of Henry Kitson, the son of William of Ashprington.

Henry, the son of William and Ann Lear, was born in Ashprington in 1737. There are no recordings relating to Henry's early life, largely because he did not go to university. He was described in the records of Torquay as a grocer of Exeter. No doubt, he was a very successful businessman who became an Alderman and Mayor of the City in 1773.

In December, 1764 he married Elizabeth, the daughter of Philip Lane, an attorney, of Crediton. They lived in 'Bury', in the parish of Lapton in Exeter. This property was purchased by Sir Richard Godwin Keats from Elizabeth, after the death of Henry in July 1795.

Henry and Elizabeth had five sons and a daughter in the space of thirteen years. Their first five children were baptised in St Mary Arches Church in Exeter while their youngest son, John Lane Kitson, born in June 1777, was baptised in Holy Trinity Church in Exeter the following year.

John Lane Kitson was educated at St Mary Hall, a part of Oriel College, Oxford. After graduating, he became a minister at Leeds in Kent and Vicar of Westleigh, near Tiverton in Devon. He was awarded an MA in 1802.

In July of that year, he married Georgiana Buller, in Exeter Cathedral. The Buller Family was one of the most influential families in the South West of England. John became Vicar of Staverton, a village north of Totnes, and then Vicar of St Andrew's Church in Ashburton the following year. He remained in Ashburton until his death in 1825. In those twenty two years, he witnessed the remarkable expansion of the town.

Ashburton has been called 'The Gateway to the Moor'. Situated on the edge of Dartmoor, the village grew into an important market town that had nearly reached its peak in the time of John Kitson.

For many years, the town, situated on the main road from London to Plymouth, as well as being associated with the tin mining in the area, was a centre for the cloth trade. Villagers, from miles around Ashburton, worked in their own homes, spinning and weaving, before coming into the town, carrying their work to the clothiers who would pay them and provide them with their raw materials to produce more cloth. The clothiers would send their cloth to the East India Company who traded with other companies in the East, particularly in China.

Then a rapid development took place when worsted spinning frames were introduced and mills were set up in and around the town. Women left their homes to work in the mills. Many people came to Ashburton to live there permanently and the population grew as a result. At the beginning of the 19th Century there were about 3000 inhabitants, a number that was to increase by a third in a short space of time.

Another change took place when Devon lost its monopoly in this trade. The East India Company changed its policy and opened up trading in the northern counties, particularly in Yorkshire. The comparatively small mills of Ashburton could not compete with the huge mills that were built in towns like Halifax and Bradford and, coupled with the economic depression of the 30s, the face of Ashburton changed yet again.

John and Georgiana's first five children were born in Ashburton. Their first son, Henry John died in March 1808 at the age of 5. Their second son, William Buller Kitson, was born in 1805 and a daughter Anne followed in 1807 before the twins, Eliza and Georgiana were born in 1810. After the birth of his twin daughters, Eliza and Georgiana, John moved to live in Crediton where three more sons and a daughter were born.

When John Lane Kitson died, his wife, Georgiana, left Crediton and moved to Paignton. It was while living there that her daughter, Eliza, married Thomas Hall and Georgiana married William Kitson in the Parish Church. Georgiana was recorded as living with her unmarried daughter, Anne, in Fisher Street on the 1841 Census.

The twins' older brother and John Lane Kitson's second son, William Buller Kitson, became a Civil Servant and moved to London. It was through William that the connection was made between William's younger sister, Eliza, and Thomas Grainger Hall where they were part of the London Society and worshipped in St George's Church, Hanover Square. No doubt part of William's family stayed with him during the 'London season'.

William married Elizabeth Ann Caird in Paignton in 1842. They lived in Chester Square and Warwick Street in West London, while he was working for HM Customs.

By 1861 William had retired and was living with his family in Vaughan Parade, Torquay, which, again, illustrates the connection between both sides of the Kitson family. His son, also named John Lane Kitson, after his grandfather, was an articled clerk in the solicitors' office of William Kitson following his education at Shrewsbury School with his brother William Thomas Kitson. While John married and lived with his wife, Charlotte, in Beaminster in Dorset where he was a successful solicitor, his brother died shortly after leaving school.

John Lane Kitson's third son, James Buller Kitson, born in Crediton in 1811, graduated from Exeter College, Oxford and later became the Vicar of Pelynt in Cornwall from 1841 until his death in 1858 when he was buried at Morval. The Church in Pelynt, a short distance from Morval, was the 'family church' of the Buller family and houses a huge memorial to generations of them.

The fourth of John and Georgiana's sons and brother of Eliza, was John Francis Howell Kitson. He was named after John's sister Ann's husband John Francis Howell, a Canon of Exeter Cathedral. He was born in Crediton in 1818 and educated at Exeter College, Oxford. He obtained his MA in 1845 before he became the Vicar of Antony in Cornwall. He was recorded on the 1851 census as being unmarried. With him was his widowed mother, Georgiana, then 73, and his sister, Ann, born in Ashburton in 1807, also unmarried, and the elder sister of the twins. They had four servants, one was 77 years old.

In 1871 Ann remained unmarried, aged 63, and living in Blindwell Cottage, Kingsteignton, where the curate was a lodger. She had witnessed the marriages of both her twin sisters.

Later John Francis Kitson married Charlotte Murray who was 29 years younger and born in Scotland. They had five sons while at the Antony Vicarage from 1871 before their daughter, Geraldine, was born in 1881. John was 63. At this time, he employed nine servants in the residence.

The Buller & Trelawny Families in Cornwall

Georgiana Buller, who married John Lane Kitson, was the daughter of William Buller and Ann Thomas of Morval in Cornwall.

William Buller's mother and, therefore, Georgiana's maternal grandmother, Rebecca, born in 1695, was the third daughter of Sir Jonathan Trelawny, born in 1650 and the Bishop of Exeter from 1689 to 1707 and of Winchester from 1707 until his death in 1721.

The Trelawny family, one of the foremost families in Cornwall, can be traced back to Saxon times but did not arrive until 1600 at their residence, 'Trelawne', near Polperro, and about a mile south east of Pelynt village. The house was built on an estate of hundreds of acres of land. The village church, originally built by the Normans, was rebuilt in the 15th century and since then many alterations and additions have taken place.

Perhaps the best known member of the family was Jonathan who was born in 1650, and was baptised in Pelynt church. He was educated at Westminster School and Christ Church College, Oxford and was ordained in 1673 before he became a royal chaplain four years later. At the age of 31, he inherited the Baronetcy on the death of his father, as well as the many debts that had been incurred in his father's earlier Royalist activities in the Civil War.

No doubt, it was his shortage of money that led him to marry a beautiful heiress, Rebecca Hele, who was just 14 years of age! She was born in Kingsteignton, the daughter of Thomas and Elizabeth Hele of 'Basombe'. Certainly his arranged marriage in 1684 helped to solve many of his problems. However, he was a loving and dutiful husband and a caring father to his thirteen children, of whom eleven survived.

He was appointed as Bishop of Bristol when he was 35 and became one of the seven bishops imprisoned in the Tower of London for refusing to implement King James II's Declaration of Indulgence granting religious tolerance to Catholics. He was tried after three weeks and acquitted.

The support which he received from the people of Cornwall led to the writing of 'The Song of the Western Men' or 'Trelawny' that has become the 'National Anthem of Cornwall':

'And shall Trelawny live?
Or shall Trelawny die!
Here's twenty thousand Cornish men
Will know the reason why!

His release is still celebrated each year on 30th June in the village of Pelynt.

King James II sought to conciliate him by the offer of the Bishopric of Exeter but Trelawny swore allegiance to William of Orange and his wife, Mary, who was King James's daughter and a staunch Protestant. He welcomed them at Torbay. Later William confirmed Jonathan's appointment as Bishop of Exeter in 1689 when he, himself, became King of England, after James had fled to France.

In 1707, Trelawny left Exeter and became the Bishop of Winchester until his death in 1721. After Sir Jonathan Trelawny died in Chelsea, his body was interred in the family vault at Pelynt Church where there are many memorials of both the Trelawny and Buller families.

One of his children, the very beautiful Rebecca, was made to marry John Francis Buller of Morval. The marriage took place in Pelynt. At that time, in July 1716, she was only 20, about the same age as John, but was distressed by the fact that her future husband's face had been badly disfigured by smallpox. In the due course of time, she became a good wife and mother!

William Buller, the son of John Francis Buller and Rebecca, was the fifth son and the youngest of their twelve children. He was born in 1735 in Morval House, their very large family residence situated north of Looe in Cornwall and only a short distance from 'Trelawne'.

William was educated at Oriel and Christ Colleges, Oxford, gaining his Masters Degree in 1759 and subsequently taking a BD and DD in 1781.

Three years later, he married Anne Thomas, daughter of John Thomas, a later Bishop of Winchester, who was also a clerk to George III. William's father-in-law helped him in the advancement of his career giving him rectories in Berkshire and Hampshire. It was while he was rector of Old Alresford that his daughter Georgiana was born in August 1777.

He was elected Dean of Exeter in 1784 and, five years later, it was in this capacity that he gave up his house near the cathedral to His Majesty King George III, Queen Charlotte and their family for their use during a visit to Exeter, as well as personally conducting a private tour of the cathedral for the royal party.

The king, grateful for the attention he had received on his visit, enabled William to move from Exeter and become Dean of Canterbury. He became a Member of The House of Lords and returned to Exeter as Bishop in 1792. This was a popular choice because of his west country background and he was made a Freeman of Exeter in the following year.

His time as Bishop was relatively short as he died, suffering from Dropsy, in December 1796 at Downes. He was interred in Exeter Cathedral. His wife, Anne, died in 1800, aged 63, and was buried near her husband.

While William's marriage played a great part in furthering his career in the Church so did that of John Lane Kitson in marrying the Bishop's daughter. John and Georgina moved from Ashburton to the 'family seat' of Downes before their son, James, was born in 1811, a year after the twins, Eliza and Georgiana, were born in Ashburton Vicarage.

Their granddaughter, Harriet, became the second wife of William Lewis Trelawny in 1872 and their family was recorded on the 1881 Census living at Trelawne Mansion. Their children were educated by a Swiss Governess in their early years. William was the 10th Baronet and a magistrate for Cornwall.

The Kitson, Buller and Trelawny families continued to inter-marry well into the 20th Century.

Trelawne Manor still stands today. The present house dates from 1650 but has been altered many times since then. Nevertheless it still conveys something of the history of the Trelawny family. The interior has been well-preserved as have the walled gardens.

The Trelawny family sold all of their estates in Cornwall in 1920. 'Trelawne' became the home of the Morley family who gave it to a charitable trust in 1945. It was used as a home for retired clergymen and their wives. By 1959 the cost of the maintenance of the estate was too great. It was sold and converted into a holiday caravan park. The house is used as office accommodation, a snooker room and a club room. The chapel is still in existence and other facilities such as swimming pools and tennis courts have been added. Everything is well-maintained in a pleasant, respected and friendly environment.

The Durant Family – 'High Canons' in Hertfordshire

Before leaving St David's in Ashprington, it may be of interest to note that outside the church is a large grave and memorial to Richard Durant who died at High Canons, near Shenley, in Hertfordshire and was buried in Ashprington in 1886.

High Canons, an estate of 800 acres, with twenty nine acres of garden, was, and remains, one of the most beautiful in the county. The house, originally built in the reign of Henry III, was later given as a retreat to the Canons of St Bartholomew's Priory in London. It passed into the hands of several notable families. The present house was built in 1773 and had three more owners before it was occupied by Mr and Mrs Thomas Fitzherbert who spent a large amount of money on the house and grounds, planting many imposing trees which, today, completely obscure a view of the house from the surrounding roads. The Fitzherberts had moved from the house by the time of Thomas' death in 1781. Four years later Maria Fitzherbert married for the third time, a marriage to the Prince Regent. She was then twenty three, six years younger than the later King George IV. Their marriage was ruled as invalid!

There were three more occupants before the estate was purchased from the MP for Leominster, Henry Bonham, in 1813 by Enosh Durant.

Who then was Enosh Durant?

Going back in time, George Durant, born about 1726 in Exeter, married Elizabeth Powell in St Mary Arches Church in Exeter in 1738. Among the five of their eight children who were born and baptised in St Edmund's Church, and who did not die in infancy, were George born in 1741 and Richard in 1752.

While Richard remained in Exeter, married Jane Pyne in 1781, and had his children baptised in Holy Trinity Church there, George moved to London where he married in 1765 in St James' Church in Westminster.

Richard's son, also Richard, born in 1791 was thus a cousin of George's son, Enosh, born in London in 1769.

Enosh's father, George, was a framework knitter who, in 1778, in partnership with John Knight, a haberdasher, became a silk broker.

Enosh began his working life as a weaver. In 1796, while living in Spital Square, he joined in partnership with John Jourdan, a silk manufacturer, who also lived in Spital Square and they too became silk brokers. Their company flourished and Enosh became extremely wealthy. He purchased the Hertfordshire property, as a country estate, for £37,000.

Enosh and his partners were highly successful in building up a very profitable business. Throughout his life, Enosh bought more and more land and buildings, adding to his Hertfordshire estate. In addition, he gave generously to a number of causes as well as being responsible, in 1840, for the building of St Peter's Church in Arkley at a cost of £5000. In addition to the church, he funded the building of an Infant School, adjoining the church. The school is now used as the church hall. Enosh built other schools in the area, one on Barnet Common in 1839 and another, an Infant School, in Shenley.

Late in his life, Enosh married 'Eliza', formerly Ann Elizabeth Trotter, in August 1839 at Brandon Hill in Bristol. He was 70 and she was 54. (Ann may have been related to John Trotter of Dyrham Park but this has not been substantiated). They leased and lived in property in Queen Anne's Street, adjoining Cavendish Square in London's West End and also retained premises in Copthall Court, Throgmorton Street in the City itself, close to the Stock Exchange.

Enosh had no children and his fortune was left to his cousin, Richard, and his heirs, providing, of course, for his own wife during her lifetime. When he died in November 1848, he was living at 12 Mansfield Street, adjacent to Queen Anne's Street where he had lived earlier. A man with very strong religious convictions, he asked to be buried, with no elaborate ceremony, in the public graveyard known as Bunhill Fields, off the City Road, and only a short distance from where he worked all of his life in London. It was here that his father, George was buried in 1802. However, a memorial plaque in St Peter's Church and parish records show that he was buried in Trinity Church,

St Marylebone.

Richard, born 23 years after his cousin, Enosh, began working as a fishmonger. In his early years, he joined Enosh in London.

In January 1821, he married Elizabeth Savage, a Londoner, who like Richard was living in the Liberty of Norton Folgate. After their marriage, they lived in Spital Square and their son, also named Richard, was born there soon afterwards. He was christened, where they had been married, in St Botolph's Church, Bishopsgate on 20th December. Later, the family moved to Copthall Court where three of their children were born and later baptised in St Andrew's Church, Holborn. They moved again and two more children were born in Leyton where they were baptised in St Mark's Church.

In August of the same year that Richard was married, he was 21, and was working in Kings Arms Yard, literally a stone's throw away from Throgmorton Street. He joined with James Pearsall, a dyer, of Cheapside, taking out a bond and also becoming a silk broker, joining his cousin's firm.

Like Enosh, Richard prospered and, in 1829, he turned to the county of his birth, buying Sharpham House and its estate adjoining the village of Ashprington in Devon while still retaining property in London.

Sharpham was a large, imposing mansion, standing in five hundred and fifty acres of parkland with a three mile frontage along the River Dart. The house was built in 1770 and the grounds, landscaped by Capability Brown, provided some of the most fantastic scenery of the river valley, as they do today.

Now there are extensive vineyards in the grounds and both wine and cheese-making are in evidence. At present, restoration work is being carried out on the property. What has been achieved so far is breathtaking. The unusual entrance hall has been beautifully restored. It is really most impressive in its oval shape, with delightful pastel pink walls and a spiral, cantilevered staircase stretching to the upper floors and finishing in a glass-domed ceiling.

Between 1829 and 1835, another son and three more daughters

were born at Sharpham. Richard donated £1,000 towards repairing St David's Church in Ashprington, and, two years later, paid for the erection of the village school at a cost of £600. He owned a large part of the parish and paid for the repair and improvement of a number of cottages and the building of the inn which was named after him.

In 1841, the Census recorded the family living on Putney Hill. At this time, their son, Richard, had also been a silk broker since 1834, when he was 21, and was living in Copthall Court. Records show that, like his father, he worked as a fishmonger during the early part of his life.

When Richard inherited High Canons in Shenley, he and members of his family lived in the mansion only occasionally. Enosh's wife would also have stayed there for some time. In 1851, at the age of 60, Richard became the High Sheriff of Devon, as well as becoming a Deputy Lieutenant of the County and a Justice of the Peace.

It appears that the younger Richard, took over 'High Canons' long before his father died in 1878 at Sharpham. In 1856, he married, Charlotte, the daughter of Colonel Alexander Wilton Dashwood of 'The Grange' in Shenley Hill, and their children were born at High Canons.

In 1863, Charlotte died, leaving five children under the age 7 living with their father. Richard lived for 23 more years, finally inheriting High Canons when his father died.

The 1871 and 1881 Censuses show Richard and his children living there. They had a butler, a footman, a groom, a house keeper and eight maids. Five years later Richard died there before being buried in Ashprington in Devon.

There were several other owners of High Canons before it was acquired by the County Council who leased the property for a variety of purposes. It was used on a number of occasions by Elstree Film Studios for film making. 'Murder on the Orient Express' and 'Half Moon Street', together with many TV shows, were made there before the property was sold again.

The Gibbs Family – Hunsdon in Hertfordshire

Richard and Charlotte Durant's daughter, Anna Maria, born in1862, married the Hon. Herbert Cokayne Gibbs, son of Henry Gibbs, Baron Aldenham, and his wife, Louisa Adams.

Herbert was born in Frognal in Hampstead, London, in 1854 and was educated at Winchester College and Trinity College, Cambridge, where he gained an MA. In 1892, following a course of training, he joined the family's merchant banking business in Bishopsgate, London.

His great grandfather, Antony, the son of an Exeter surgeon, founded the family business in 1808, engaging in merchant banking. The firm originally had connections with Spain but, by 1820, it had adopted the west coast of South America for its trading. Guano, used in the making of fertilisers, became its main interest from 1842, as Antony Gibbs & Sons Ltd became a prominent City merchant bank. Their business changed into financing the production and trading in new nitrate fertilisers and Herbert was sent to Valpariso to supervise investments. After 1881 the bank became involved in shipping, import trading and mining. Herbert became the key figure in the company from 1900 to 1933. He was responsible for the nitrate side of the business, which became the supplier of thousands of tons of nitrate required by the Ministry of Munitions in the First World War. His involvement in the supply and demand, and the organisation and accounting of this, as director of purchases for Europe, led the French government to confer on him the Légion d'honneur in 1918, a time when his bank had reached its peak.

The Gibbs family were proud of being united, working and living for one another. Their beliefs helped them enormously in their endeavours and their business proved to be very successful. However, it was the inheritance of land from the Hucks family that made Herbert and his father wealthy.

Herbert purchased properties in Hertfordshire in 1909. His main acquisition was 'Briggens Mansion' with its lodge and park, situated north-east of Roydon and north of Harlow. At the same time, he bought nearby Brickhouse Farm, with 211 acres of land, and 'Hunsdon Mill House' overlooking the River Stort. In addition, he acquired the 'sporting rights' of the park and plantation of 'Hunsdon House' situated north of 'Briggens'. The family estates amounted to 3035 acres in Hertfordshire, 1309 acres in Oxfordshire and 128 acres in Middlesex and Berkshire.

Herbert and his family lived in London in Portman Square, St Marylebone. The 1911 census recorded Herbert and Anna Maria with their family of six children, three sons and three daughters, born between 1886 and 1902. They employed two footmen, a butler, a cook, a nurse and seven maids to care for them. Of course, 'Briggens' was used as their country residence.

His purchase of 'Briggens' led to Herbert becoming interested in social history and he published a number of works dealing with genealogy, as well as those on currency and taxation. His interest in local history, as well as his extensive recordings of the peerage, resulted in his publication in 1915, 'The Parish Register of Hunsdon' and, in 1925, 'The History of Gibbs in Fenton, in Dartington'. This was a branch of his family living close to where his wife's family had their country estate at Sharpham, Devon, both having their roots in Exeter.

Active on behalf of the Conservative Party, Herbert was Chairman of the City of London Conservative Association from 1912 to 1932 and from 1924 to 1932 he was a founder and president of the 1912 Club. He shared his political interest with his wife who was president of the women's branch of the association. In 1918 she and her daughters formed the Women's Institute in Hunsdon. It was the second such institute in Hertfordshire.

Herbert held the office of High Sheriff of Hertfordshire in 1913 and was a Justice of the Peace in the county. In July 1923 he was created 1st Baron Hunsdon of Hunsdon and Anna Maria received the title Baroness Hunsdon of Hunsdon. Herbert died, following a short illness, in May 1935 and was buried in St Dunstan's Church. Anna Maria lived for another four years and is believed to have died at 'Hunsdon Mill House' before being buried with her husband.

Although receiving the title Baron Hunsdon of Hunsdon, Herbert did not live in Hunsdon House.

'Hunsdon House', built in 1447 by Sir William Oldhall, became a great Tudor house when it was developed by Henry VIII in 1525. It was used by the king, largely because of the excellent hunting facilities it offered as well as being a haven to escape the threat of the plague in London. His children, Edward, Mary and Elizabeth spent much of their time there in their early years and Prince Edward spent a great deal of his youth living there. In 1548, after his father had died, Edward gave Hunsdon to his sister, Mary. When Elizabeth became Queen Elizabeth I, she created the Lordship of Hunsdon for her cousin, Sir Henry Carey, the son of Mary Boleyn, in 1559. From that time, much of the original building was pulled down and re-built and only a small part of Henry's great Tudor house remained by the beginning of the 19th Century. It fell into disrepair in early Victorian times but further renovations and additions were carried out about 1860. The present castle-like structure, flying the flag of St George of England, remains very impressive, although it is less than a quarter the size of the original. It stands in formal gardens and parkland behind the church of St Dunstan in Acorn Street, Hunsdon.

Herbert Gibbs pointed out that St Dunstan's was probably the only village church in England in which four successive monarchs had regularly worshipped within its walls.

In recent years, 'Briggens' has been used as an hotel with an adjoining golf course. Although the golf course is still used, the house itself has fallen into serious disrepair and, although there are intentions to refurbish the property, planning applications being made in 2002, it would appear to be an unlikely project.

The Trotter Family – 'Dyrham Park' in Hertfordshire

Louisa Blanche, the daughter of Richard Durant of 'High Canons', married John, the son of John Trotter of 'Dyrham Park' on 21st July, 1886 at Shenley.

Mary Elizabeth, another daughter of Richard Durant, married Frederick, the son of John Trotter of 'Dyrham Park' at Shenley on 10th February, 1887.

'Dyrham Park' is between the A1 and the A1081, Barnet to St. Alban's Road. The estate is approached from the main road by way of a minor road named Trotters Bottom or the less obviously named Galley Lane.

The Dyrham Park estate, originally Durham Park, was the home of John Durham in the 14th Century. The manor house is now a Palladian mansion which has a magnificent dining hall, adjoining reception rooms and a minstrels' gallery, together with an impressive stairway to the bedrooms on the upper floor. Additions have been made to the original building and there are now rooms on a second floor extension.

The house, situated in 200 acres of simply delightful grounds, was originally accessed from the north of the park by way of a spectacular gateway which may or may not have been built to celebrate the coronation of King Charles II and transported to 'Dyrham Park' at a much later stage.

Several generations of well-known Hertfordshire families, such as the Frowkes and the Keppels lived here before the Trotters.

John Trotter purchased the property in 1798. He was one of at least five children born to Archibald Trotter and Jean Mowbray.

Shortly after John moved to 'Dyrham Park', the old house was destroyed by fire and the present house was rebuilt on the same site.

On 28th July 1804, John married Felicity Swinton and their son, also named John, was born four years later. He had two brothers and two sisters.

John served as a captain in the 2nd Life Guards. He succeeded his father in 1833 at which time he married the Honourable Charlotte Amelia Liddell, daughter of the 1st Baron Ravensworth of County Durham.

John and Charlotte had eleven children, including twins, all born at 'Dyrham Park'. All of their six sons lived over the age of 59, married and produced fifteen children between them. Their six daughters all married and, with one exception, lived to be over 55. They had twenty children and John and Charlotte had, at least, 58 recorded grandchildren.

When John died in October, 1870 he was buried in the grounds of St Margaret's Church, Ridge, where he and his family worshipped together with the Ebbs family who lived in the village of Ridge.

There is a decorated sarcophagus, enclosed by railings, which is a memorial to him and to several members of the Trotter family. As well as the inscriptions for John, there are those for Charlotte his wife, his son Frederick and his wife, Mary Elizabeth, the daughter of Richard Durant.

In another grave was buried John's daughter, Jean, the wife of Sir Algernon Coote. She died in 1880 at the age of 35.

John's son, Edward who died in 1903 and his wife, Annie, who died in 1920 were also buried close by.

Finally, John's son, John of 'Brickendon Grange' and his wife, Louisa, the daughter of Richard Durant, were buried there in 1913 and 1922.

Several almshouses built in the village in 1844 at the express wish of Jean Trotter have now been converted into one dwelling house, 'Orchard Mead', but the building remains as a constant reminder of Jean, born in 1816, the daughter of John and Felicity and sister of Captain John Trotter.

Frederick, the son of John and Charlotte Trotter

John and Charlotte's eldest son, Frederick, born in 1838, also joined the Army. He served in the 39th (Dorsetshire) Regiment and was an ensign in June 1858, a lieutenant in May 1862 and a captain in May 1867 serving for ten years. He inherited the Dyrham Park estate when his father died in 1870.

At the age of 49 in 1887, he was the last of John's children to marry. He and his wife, Mary Elizabeth Durant, had four children. Two died in infancy.

In 1901, Mary remained, as a widow, living at 'Dyrham Park' with her son, Frederick Liddell Trotter, aged 3, and her daughter, Eleanor, aged 7.

A staff of seven lived in the house, including a footman. In cottages within the grounds there were a coachman, a groom and several gardeners, as well as their families.

Ten years later, Eleanor, was still living at 'Dyrham Park' with her mother, who employed a governess from Strasbourg to educate her daughter. There was a cook, together with a footman and five maids 'living in' while a large staff continued to care for the grounds.

Mary sent her son, Frederick Liddell to a boys' boarding school. He was at Stone House on the North Foreland of Broadstairs in Kent.Later he became a Major in the Army and married Evelyn, the daughter of Brigadier General R S Oxley CB CMG DSO of Queen Camel House near Yeovil in Somerset.

Their daughter, Eleanor, remained unmarried and lived to be 75.

John, the son of John and Charlotte Trotter

Frederick's brother, John, born in 1854, was sent to school at Repton. He was recorded on the 1881 census with his brother, Stuart, three years older, living at 'Laurel Lodge'. Stuart was the manager of the Soho Bazaar, said to be the finest of the Victorian Bazaars in London and situated in Soho Square off Oxford Street, while John was described as a Swedish Merchant.

'Laurel Lodge' was built on land owned by the Trotter family and was situated off Dancers Hill Road, not more than a hundred yards from the main entrance to Dyrham Park.

The building, again in the Palladian style, was very impressive. It was situated in eight acres of beautiful grounds and the brothers employed a butler, a footman, a groom, a housekeeper and three maids, together with a coachman and his family who lived in a cottage in the grounds. The house was approached by a long winding drive and was totally secluded.

In more recent times 'Laurel Lodge' has been developed into a luxurious property, described as 'an ambassadorial style family residence, thought to be valued at nearly £10,000,000.' It has a marbled entrance hall, an elegant staircase leading to the en-suite bedrooms. There is an indoor swimming pool, a squash court, a gym and a cinema. The kitchen, dining room and two reception rooms are on the ground floor. One reception room measures approximately 48ft by 31ft.

The path is now illuminated and passes tennis courts and a lake. There is an ornate fountain in front of the main entrance which is thought to have been there when the property was built.

In 1886, John married Louisa Blanche Durant in Shenley and they lived in 'Brickendon Grange', near Bayford.

They were there in 1891 with their son, Richard, aged 3, their daughter, Agnes, aged 2 and son, Colin, aged 1. They employed a butler, a cook, a nurse and three maids, as well as two gardeners. John was still a Swedish merchant but also the director of an insurance company.

Ten years later, in 1901, the family was recorded living at their London address, 1 Hyde Park Street in Paddington when John was described as a solicitor. Agnes was 13 and another son, Kenneth, was 8 and a daughter, Lova, was 3.

The family was recorded back at Brickendon on the 1911 census when John and Louisa had been married for 25 years. John was shown as a bank director who employed a domestic staff of seven, together with a governess.

Their daughter, Agnes, was 22 and unmarried and their other daughter, Lova, was 13. At this time their son, Colin, aged 21, was an undergraduate at Trinity College, Cambridge

Their sons, Richard and Kenneth were not with them.

Two years later, John died, just before the outbreak of the First World War. Louisa lived through it and experienced the loss of her sons before she died in 1922.

Richard became a Captain in the Army and served in the First World War. In 1921, he was living in 'Brickendon Grange'. In December, 1923, the property was sold to Lt. Col. Kenneth Rankin Campbell DSO.

Richard's brother, Colin Liddell Trotter, was a Lieutenant, who was killed in the First World War as was his brother, Kenneth Stuart Trotter who was killed in action in 1915 while serving in the 2nd

Light Rifle Brigade. He was 22.

In 1844, John Trotter bought a piece of land, a very small amount of George Byng's 2,500 acres of 'Wrotham Park', situated between Kitts End Road and the Great North Road. On the estate, which has belonged to the Byng family since 1754, stands another very large Palladian mansion. Today it is used for private receptions, conferences and celebrations much in the same way as 'Dyrham Park'.

It is said John Trotter paid £70 for the site. He commissioned the architect, Gilbert Scott, to design a church for the site. At first a minister's house and a school were erected and then Christ Church, built with flint stones, first used as a chapel-of-ease, opened in 1845. It was consecrated in 1852.

The living was endowed by John Trotter with £1,000 and was a perpetual curacy until 1898 when the full rights of a vicar were granted to the incumbent. In 1919 the patronage of the Trotter family ended.

The first incumbent was Alfred Moyes, a converted Jew, who served there as the curate for seven years. He was followed by William Pennefather, a close friend of John Trotter.

During his time at the church William Pennefather welcomed another friend on several occasions. He was David Livingstone who was staying at Hadley Green from 1957 to 1958 while writing a book. In 1858 he returned to Africa to explore more of the Zambesi river and discover Lake Nyasa.

William Pennefather's ministry ended in 1864 when he became Vicar of St Jude's Church in Mildmay Park. His work there in putting his life at risk to help to fight an outbreak of cholera in London is well-documented. He, and a team of women, known as 'deaconesses', visited the sick in their own homes.

William died in 1873 and was buried in the church grounds at Ridge with John Trotter who had worked with him to establish the Mildmay Mission. This was the first medical mission hospital and was opened in 1877, four years after William's death, and moved to its present site in Hackney Road in 1892.

A building adjoining Christ Church and called the 'Pennefather Memorial Hall' was erected in 1907 and illustrates how much his work was appreciated. He achieved so much in Barnet.

His ministry was followed by that of John Trotter's son, Henry, who did not remain in Barnet for any length of time as, in 1881, he was the vicar of St Andrew the Less in Cambridge and was living in the vicarage of Christ Church with his wife and their seven year old daughter, Grace. Ten years later, he was the rector of Trowbridge in Wiltshire.

Another of Frederick's brothers, Mowbray, born in 1849, became the rector of St Mary de Crypt in Littleworth, Gloucester. He was recorded with his wife and his mother, Charlotte, on the 1881 Census living in the rectory in Brunswick Square, Gloucester.

His younger brother, Stuart, noted above, born in 1852, became a Land Agent. He married in 1886. His wife, Mary Ellen Gladstone, was born in Highfield, Manchester. In 1901 he was living at Hill Farm in Wormley, Hertfordshire with his wife, one son and one daughter. Ten years later they were living in 'Broomfield Lodge', Chelmsford.

By this time, they had two sons and three daughters living with them. One son was a civil engineer and the other was an Oxford undergraduate. Among the eight members of their domestic staff was a governess for their younger daughter, Muriel, aged 6. Unusually, a 31 year old masseuse was also employed by them and living in the house. This may indicate an infirmity in the family.

In 1938 'Dyrham Park' was owned by Hertfordshire County Council and in the early 1960's it was converted into a Golf and Country Club in a truly magnificent setting.

As well as an 18-hole golf course, there is a practice ground of seven acres. There is now a large outdoor, heated swimming pool surrounded by sunbeds! There are tennis courts, a snooker room and card rooms for the use of the members. Parties, banquets and wedding celebrations are frequently held in the magnificent dining room and charity days are a feature of the club activities.

The Bevan Family – 'Trent Park' in Hertfordshire

Perhaps of greater interest in showing family connections in Hertfordshire was the marriage of John Trotter's daughter Maria, the sister of Frederick. On 1st July 1875, she became the third wife of Francis Augustus Bevan.

The Bevan family were Quakers who originally came from the Swansea area of Wales.

Silvanus Bevan, born in 1661, was a burgess of the City of Swansea. He married Jane Phillips when he was 24 and had five sons and six daughters. He possessed farmlands and estates. He suffered persecution from the Puritans and Anglicans for his religious beliefs and, together with others of the many Quaker families in the area, like the Barclays and the Gurneys, he gave his support to the Duke of Beaufort and managed the Duke's interests until his death in 1725.

His eldest son Silvanus, born in 1691, left Wales and, as a young man, served an apprenticeship as an apothecary in Cheapside, London. When he gained his 'freedom' in 1715 he established a pharmacy at 2, Plough Court, in Lombard Street which he rented from a Quaker merchant.

In the same year, Silvanus Bevan married Elizabeth, the daughter of Daniel Quare, the clockmaker to George I. The Duchess of Marlborough, Lord Finch and William Penn attended the marriage ceremony which took place in the Quaker Meeting House in Gracechurch Street and afterwards a banquet was held in the Skinners Hall. Elizabeth died in childbirth a year later and Silvanus married again in 1719. The marriage was childless.

In 1725 he expanded his business by taking over the lease of 3 Plough Court. In that year he was elected to the Fellowship of the Royal Society.

His younger brother, Timothy, joined him in the business and was elected as a member of the Society of Apothecaries when he gained his 'freedom' in 1730.

Timothy married Elizabeth Barclay of Swansea five years later and their two sons, Timothy and Silvanus, were taken into partnership

Ridge Church, South Mimms

Dyrham Park in Barnet – front elevation

Dyrham Park in Barnet – rear elevation

Allen & Hanbury's factory in Ware

Hunsdon Mill

Bevan Family Grave, Christ Church, Cockfosters

Hunsdon Church

Hunsdon Churchyard & Palace

Tyttenhanger Park, London Colney

Sydney Lodge, Humble, Hampshire

Sydney Lodge Stable Block

in the business off Lombard Street, after the death of the founder, Silvanus, who, for the latter part of his life, left Plough Court and worked as a physician from his home in Hackney. He died in 1765 and was buried in Bunhill Fields.

Timothy's son, Silvanus, did not remain in the business choosing a career in banking with his uncle, James Barclay.

Timothy Bevan & Son had grown into a respected pharmaceutical business when William Allen joined the firm in 1792.

William, born in 1770, in Spitalfields, London, was the son of devout Quakers. At an early age he became interested in science and had no wish to follow his father into the silk business. In 1795 he was made a partner in the Bevans' business and, two years later, he became the sole owner of the company.

In 1806 William married Charlotte Hanbury, the daughter of another affluent Quaker family, his first wife, Mary, having died in childbirth. The Hanbury family had several important scientists among its members.

In 1808 William's nephew, Daniel Hanbury, joined the pharmacy business and in 1824 Daniel and his cousin, Cornelius Hanbury, were taken into partnership, the name of the business changing to Allen & Hanbury.

William became highly successful and had a large circle of friends, including Elizabeth Fry. Outside of his scientific interests, he was a passionate believer in the Abolition of Slavery and worked unceasingly in this cause, following in the work of Wilberforce and Clarkson.

In 1841, he became the founder of the Pharmaceutical Society and was its first president.

On Allen's death in September 1843, at the age of 73, the Hanbury family ran the pharmaceutical business. In the second half of the 19th century the company opened factories in Ware in Hertfordshire and in Bethnal Green in London.

In the 1870s, the company's main products were cod liver oil, throat pastilles, rusks and milk food for infants. In 1893 the company was registered as being wholesale and retail chemists.

Allen & Hanbury's food for healthy living became world famous, its products being sold as The 'Allenburys' Foods.

In 1923 the company started to produce Insulin and its annual turnover reached £1,000,000. It went on to produce a range of surgical instruments and hospital equipment.

Glaxo acquired the company in 1958 but Allen & Hanbury's name was retained. In 1968 it produced the Ventolin spray (Salbutamol) which was a life saving development for many people suffering from asthma and other breathing difficulties.

Glaxo merged with Smith & Kline to become one of the four largest manufacturing chemists in the world. The GSK factory, overlooking the river in Ware, still retains the Allen & Hanbury's sign above one entrance. Now the factory is massive, as new buildings have been added to the original construction on a regular basis, and covers acres of ground. Nevertheless, today, Ware is considered one of GSK's smaller concerns.

Timothy Bevan's son, Silvanus, born in 1743, as stated above, did not follow him into the pharmaceutical trade but became a banker. He joined a Quaker goldsmith and banking firm founded by John Freame in 1728. Freame's brother in law, James Barclay, Silvanus's uncle, became a partner in 1736 and two of his relatives, Silvanus Bevan and John Tritton joined in 1762 and 1767 respectively to establish Barclays, Bevan and Tritton, later to be just Barclays Bank, which prospered until the existence of private banks was threatened by new legislature in the late 19th Century.

Silvanus' first wife, Isabella, the daughter of Edward Wakefield, a mercer who lived in Kensington and who came from an old Westmoreland Quaker family, died of fever after 7 months of married life in November 1769.

In 1773 he married for a second time. Louisa was the daughter of Henry Kendall, a banker of Lincoln's Inn Fields in London. She was not a Quaker and Silvanus was obliged to leave the Society of Friends.

He and Louisa had seven sons. The oldest, David, was born in 1774 in Bishopsgate. He also became a banker and was made a partner in Barclay, Bevan & Co of Lombard Street in the City of London. In 1798, he married Favell Bourke, the daughter of Robert Cooper Lee of Berners Street and Bedford Square in London and of Rosehall in Jamaica.

At the time of their marriage, David was 23 and Favell was 17. She had just completed a five year course at Miss Olier's School in Bloomsbury Square, London, when the marriage was arranged. They lived in the Bank premises in Lombard Street before moving to accommodation in Upper Guildford Street and then to Russell Square. They moved to York Place before settling in a large house, 'Hale End' in Walthamstow in 1808. While living in this area, they were able to enjoy the 'London Season' as well as becoming a part of the social scene in Paris and Brussels.

This property was sold after they had lived there for about 14 years. Subsequently they moved to 42 Upper Harley Street in London. They also owned Fosbury House in Wiltshire.

David's son, Robert Cooper Lee Bevan was born in 1809 while the family was living in Walthamstow. He was educated at Harrow and Trinity College, Oxford.

In 1826 David Bevan bought a house called 'Mount Pleasant' in Cockfosters. Previously the house, built by Inigo Jones, had been owned by several families of note. Sir William Henry Ashurst, Justice of the King's Bench, sold it to William Franks in 1786. Four years later, it was owned by William Wroughton, His Majesty's Surveyor of Woods for the Duchy of Lancaster, before it was the home of David Bevan. The name of the house was changed to 'Belmont' and it was enlarged considerably during his occupancy.

In the same year in which Robert finished his education at Harrow, before matriculating at Trinity College, Oxford, David Bevan had to withdraw from the management of the bank after a paralytic seizure. Shortly after this, Robert, left Oxford without a degree as the condition of his father worsened. Robert took over David's place as a partner in the bank.

In 1846, David Bevan, who had been partially paralysed for twenty years, died following a tragic accident. After having breakfast, he began reading his mail. He had moved towards the fire for extra warmth when his dressing gown caught alight. His butler heard a bell ring and moved quickly to the breakfast room, only to find David engulfed in flames. He threw him to the ground and rolled him in a rug, attempting to put out the fire. In spite of extensive burns, David insisted on going to his room following the accident. He died shortly afterwards. He was buried in the Bevan family vault built by his son, Robert, in 1838 at Christ Church, Cockfosters. His property 'Belmont' was occupied by Henry Alexander, an East India director, who lived in the house until his death in 1861 when he was aged 73. He was buried in the graveyard of Christ Church, Cockfosters, and the property was purchased by Charles Addington Hanbury of the family living at 'Poles' in Thundridge, Hertfordshire (Hanbury Manor).

In 1833 David Bevan had bought the 'Trent Park' estate for his son, Robert, who used this as his country home, together with the family estate in Wiltshire and houses in London and Brighton, for more than 50 years. Robert owned nearly four thousand acres of land.

He married Lady Agneta Elizabeth Yorke in 1836. Lady Agneta was the great granddaughter of the first Earl of Hardwicke and her father, Sir Joseph Sydney Yorke, KCB was a Vice-Admiral. One brother was the MP for Cambridge while another was Archdeacon of Huntingdon , Canon of Ely and rector of Wimpole in Cambridge. In a distinguished career, her father's uncle was Solicitor General and Lord High Chancellor of Great Britain.

The family home was Wimpole Hall, some five miles north of Royston on the Hertfordshire/ Cambridge border. At the time of her marriage, Lady Agneta's address was Sydney Lodge in Hampshire.

In 1838/9 Robert paid for the building of Trent School for girls and infants in Chalk Lane, Cockfosters, as well as funding a church in close proximity. The church, Trent Church, later became known as Christ Church, Cockfosters.

At a later date a boys' school, built on another site on the other side of the main Cockfosters Road, amalgamated with the girls' school which was rebuilt at the same time in 1957 and became Trent Church of England Primary School.

Robert's son, Francis Bevan was born in 1840 in Upper Harley Street, London and was the second son of fourteen children of Robert Bevan. His mother, Lady Agneta Yorke, died when Francis was 10. She had four sons and two daughters. At the age of 18, Francis became a partner in Barclays Bank.

In 1856, Robert married Emma Frances, born in Oxford in 1827, the eldest of three daughters born to Philip Shuttleworth, Warden of New College, Oxford, for eighteen years before becoming Bishop of Chichester. Emma Frances was living with her widowed mother at Wykenham Rise in Totteridge when she met Robert. She and Robert had eight children who grew into adulthood.

Emma Frances joined the Plymouth Brethren shortly after her marriage and withdrew from society life. She wore black and became increasingly reclusive. Her children received a very strict upbringing. She was highly intellectual, spoke French and German, and worked as a translator and writer of religious works.

Her husband, Robert, remained an Anglican but shared his wife's strict religious attitudes to life. He organised daily prayer meetings at the bank's offices in Lombard Street. He gave up hunting which he had enjoyed in earlier times, and continued to spend large sums of money on church building and on donating to charities.

In 1862, Robert's son, Francis, married Elizabeth Marianne, the daughter of Lord Charles James Fox Russell. They had one son, Cosmo, born in May 1863. Elizabeth died less than a fortnight later. She was 22.

Francis married for a second time in 1866. His wife was Constance Hogg, the youngest daughter of Sir James Weir Hogg, baronet.

In 1871, Francis and Constance were living at 72 Princes Gate, Kensington. Francis and Elizabeth's son, Cosmo, aged 7, was with them as well as four of Constance's young sons. The census reveals that they had a staff of ten, including a butler and a footman. Constance died after the birth of another son in 1872. She was 31.

In 1875 Francis married Maria Trotter and they had two daughters.

Their younger daughter, Audrey, married Lionel Micklem who was born in 1873 in Abbots Mead, Elstree (see notes on Stanley Kubrick and the Cowell family).

Prior to 1890, as well as living in London, Francis lived in 'Ludgrove Hall' in Hadley Wood, Barnet, which was part of the Trent estate that had been purchased by the Bevan family. This early 19th century stuccoed building stood on a site where building had taken place in 1596 and, of which, there were no remains. In the later part of the century extensions were made to the house and, again, more red brick building was added in the 20th century.

On 22nd July 1890 Robert Bevan died, aged 81, having suffered from gout and other debilitating illnesses. The gross value of his estate was estimated to be worth over £950,000.

Francis and Maria lived in the 'Trent Park Mansion' itself after Robert's death. Maria died in 1903 and the Trent estate was sold to Sir Edward Sassoon in 1909.

Francis lived in Tilney Street, Mayfair after this time. He died in 'Monk Sherbourne', Granville Road, Eastbourne in Sussex in August 1919 having suffered from heart disease for some time. He was buried in the family grave at Christ Church, Cockfosters. His estate was less than half of that of his father, due to his generosity towards a large number of Christian charities and missions.

Ludgrove Hall, where Francis had lived until 1890, was sold to Arthur Dunn in 1892 when it was used as a boys' boarding school.

Arthur Tempest Blakiston Dunn was born in Whitby in 1860. He was educated at Eton and Cambridge.

In 1891 he and his family were living in Kirby Lodge in the village of Little Shelford in the Chesterton District of Cambridgeshire. Arthur's father, John, taught Latin, Greek and Mathematics in the University where Arthur worked as a tutor in Trinity College.

Arthur became an outstanding amateur footballer, playing for the Old Etonians, Corinthian Casuals and Cambridge University. He played in two Cup Finals for the Old Etonians at Kennington Oval and also played four times as an amateur international for England.

His boarding school was recorded on the 1901 Census when he was shown with his wife, Helen, and their children, John, Marjory and Olive as well as sixty 'boarders' between the ages of 8 and 13. Living in the Hall were two nurses and a domestic staff of twelve.

In addition, six assistant schoolmasters lived in adjoining accommodation, as well as a matron, a gardener and his family, and three laundry maids.

Among his pupils were Osbert Sitwell and Alec Douglas Hume, another future British Prime Minister, as well as Clement Attlee, to be educated in a Hertfordshire 'prep' school.

Arthur died in February 1902, aged 41. After his death, the 'Arthur Dunn Cup' was created in his memory. The trophy was awarded to the winning team of a 'knock out' football competition which involved former pupils of leading independent or 'public schools' taking part.

After 1939 Ludgrove was used by the War Office as an interrogation centre for high ranking enemy air force officers who became 'prisoners of war'. Other prisoners were held there at a later stage.

It became a hostel for those training to be teachers at Trent Park when this became a teachers training college after the Second World War.

In the 1890s, Henry Frampton Stallard, an Indian Army officer founded Heddon Court Preparatory School in Hampstead. In 1920, the school moved to 'Belmont' in Cockfosters. The property was enlarged even more and its name was changed to Heddon Court.

John Betjeman, later to become the Poet Laureate, taught at the school for a year, from April 1929 to July 1930. He was appointed as 'The Cricket Master', the subject of one of his poems. Previously he had taught for a short while at Thorpe House School in Gerrard's Cross following his 'inglorious departure' from Oxford.

In 1933, the Belmont estate was sold to developers. Building was postponed during the war years but was completed in 1948. The area where 'Belmont' stood is now covered by 'town houses' and there is no longer any evidence of Belmont Farm which formed a part of the surrounding area. All that remains as a memory of the past are the names of the roads – Heddon Court Parade, Heddon Court Avenue,

Heddon Road, Mount Pleasant and Bevan Road.

Barclays took on a new form when it merged with 20 other private banks, largely Quaker based organisations (see Hitchin notes and the Lucas Family). Barclay & Co Ltd., became a joint stock association and Silvanus Bevan's grandson, Francis Bevan became a partner in 1859 at the age of 18. He became a senior partner when his father died in 1890 and six years later he was the new chairman. He served in this capacity for 20 years until his retirement at the beginning of 1917 having given his entire working life to Barclays bank. His son, Cosmo, followed into the bank and became a director in 1905. He was Vice Chairman from 1917 to 1918 and retired in 1934. Francis's younger brother, Wilfred Arthur Bevan, became a director of Barclays in 1896 and remained as such until his death in 1905.

Barclays was, until quite recently, run by local directors born into families of considerable standing, usually Quakers, who exerted immense power even when they were not majority shareholders. Partners, as seen, were appointed from within families and promotion depended on social status and family connections rather than ability, achievement or initiative. The names of Tuke, Barclay, Bevan, Goodenough, Seebohm and Tritton appear with others throughout the history of the bank in high managerial positions.

The Yorke Family – Hamble-Le-Rice in Hampshire

Lady Agneta Yorke, who married Robert Bevan of Trent Park, was a great granddaughter of Philip Yorke, the first Earl of Hardwicke.

Philip Yorke was born in 1690 in Dover, the son of Philip Yorke, a barrister. He showed exceptional academic promise in his early education and was entered into an attorney's office in London. His employer entered him at the Middle Temple in 1708. In 1715 he was called to the bar where he made rapid progress. He entered parliament in 1719 and was appointed solicitor-general at the age of twenty-nine and received a knighthood in 1720, although he was then a barrister with only four years standing.

In 1719 he married Margaret Cocks and had five sons and two daughters.

At the age of forty two, he was a peer and chief justice and, in 1737, he was appointed Lord Chancellor until his resignation in 1756, becoming the longest serving chancellor in the 18th century. In spite of resigning from this post, he remained an effective part of the government of this country until 1762.

In 1739 he purchased Wimpole Hall, the largest country house in Cambridgeshire, just outside of Royston in Hertfordshire.

He became the first Earl of Hardwicke in 1754 and was also made Viscount Royston in that year. He died in 1764 and was succeeded by his son, Philip, who became the second earl. Philip married Lady Jemima Campbell and they had two daughters.

On his death in 1790, the title passed to his nephew, Philip, who became the third Earl of Hardwicke. Philip was the son of Charles Yorke, the second son of the first earl.

Charles married Catherine Freeman in 1755. She was the only child and heiress of the Reverend William Freeman of 'Aspeden (Aspenden) Hall' near Buntingford in Hertfordshire. The Freeman family had been closely connected with the church of St Mary Aspeden from the 17th century after William and Ralph Freeman, London merchants, had bought the manor in 1608.

Catherine's father died in 1749 and so she inherited 'Aspenden Hall', where she remained with her mother, before she married Charles Yorke in 1755.

Her mother was Catherine Blount, daughter of Sir Thomas Pope Blount as well as being the sister and eventual heiress of Sir Harry Pope Blount, 3rd Baronet of 'Tyttenhanger Park', close to London Colney in Hertfordshire.

The Tyttenhanger manor house was built in 1654. It was a rectangular red-brick building with a tiled roof. Its chimneys were plain but massive. On the ridge of the roof was a large square wooden clock turret. Inside there was a particularly impressive, elaborately carved, oak staircase which rose from the ground floor to the attic rooms. It can still be seen today.

Two years after her husband died, her brother, Sir Harry, died without issue and she eventually inherited part of his estates. The family were closely attached to St Margaret's Church in Ridge and, in his will, Sir Harry expressed his desire to be buried in the family grave there.

Both the Ebbs and the Durant families worshipped in the same church and had family graves in the churchyard. Joseph Ebbs worked as a bailiff at Tyttenhanger for the Boult family. The Boult Family have an altar tomb in the church on the north side of the chancel within the communion rails.

Two years after, in 1759, Catherine, then Catherine Yorke, died and Charles became a widower, having their child, Philip, to care for.

In 1762, he married for the second time. His wife was Agneta Johnson, daughter and co-heiress of Henry Johnson of Great Berkhamstead in Berkshire. Charles and Agneta had four sons and one daughter. It is thought that Agneta returned to Great Berkhamstead for the birth of her children. The family lived in 'Aspenden Hall' and 'Tyttenhanger Park', as well as having a residence in London.

Charles had a distinguished legal and political career but died at the age of forty-eight in 1770, just three days after being appointed as Lord Chancellor. His death was said to have been brought about by political pressure.

The title of 3rd Earl of Hardwicke passed to Philip Yorke, the son of Charles Yorke and the former husband of Catherine Freeman. He and his wife, Lady Elizabeth Lindsay, had two sons and four daughters but, by the time Philip died in 1834, both his sons had died and so the title of 4th Earl passed to Sir Joseph's eldest son, Charles.

It was Philip Yorke who arranged for the building of 'Sydney Lodge' on the Solent Estuary. Agneta had been widowed after seven years of marriage to Charles, and wanted somewhere new to spend her life.

The area chosen was Hamble, in Hampshire, one of the smallest villages in England at that time. The village situated on the Solent, was in an area where other members of the family lived and had strong naval connections.

Sydney Lodge was built between 1789 and 1798, designed by Sir John Soane, the highly regarded architect who had designed the Bank of England. He had worked on both 'Aspenden House' and 'Tyttenhanger Park', carrying out renovations and enlargements to the properties for the Yorke family.

The Lodge, built on high ground outside of the village of Hamble and overlooking the Solent, was a red-brick rectangular building with a central entrance and a stepped porch supported by circular pillars. Everything about the building was absolutely symmetrical. It had a ground and one upper floor, with attic rooms above, having dormer windows in the tiled roof and equidistant chimneys.

Agneta moved to 'Sydney Lodge' in the early 1790's and she remained there nearly until the time of her death. She actually died in Bath in 1820 where she had probably been staying for health reasons.

Her son, Joseph, moved into 'Sydney Lodge, two years before, in 1818, but he had had close links with the area long before this time.

Joseph had joined the Navy as a young boy of eleven and served for over fifty years, rising through the ranks with great distinction, both in war and peacetime. He became a Vice-Admiral.

He married Elizabeth Rattray in 1798. She was the daughter of James Rattray of Atherston. They had four sons and a daughter.

The youngest child, a daughter, named Agneta after her grandmother, was born in December, 1811, and baptised in the following month at St Martin's in The Fields in London.

Her mother, Elizabeth, died three weeks later.

In 1813 her father married Lady Urania Kington, daughter of the 12th Lord Winchester. She was the widow, firstly of the Marquess of Clanricarde and, secondly, of Colonel Peter Kington who died in 1807.

Sir Joseph retired from the Admiralty in 1818 having been made a KCB three years before. However his work in the Navy did not end then. From 1790 he also served as a Member of Parliament representing both Reigate and Sandwich until his death.

He was made an admiral in 1830. On 5th May, 1831 Joseph and three other seamen were returning to Hamble in a fourteen ton yacht, having visited a flagship moored off Spithead, when their vessel was struck by lightning, causing it to capsize. All four seamen drowned in Stokes Bay. Joseph, who appeared to have been struck by the lightening, was buried in the family vault in Hamble churchyard.

One of Agneta's brothers, the Ven. Hon. Henry Yorke, was Archdeacon of Huntingdon, Canon of Ely and rector of Wimpole in Cambridge.

Her brother Eliot Yorke DL, became the MP for Cambridge. He married Emily Delme-Radcliffe of the family who owned Hitchin Priory and so forged another link with Hertfordshire. The Hon. Mrs Eliot Yorke lived in a house called 'Hamble Cliff' near Netley Hospital.

Although the ancestral home of the Yorke family was seen as Wimpole Hall, at the time of her marriage to Robert Lee Cooper Bevan in 1836, Lady Agneta's address was given as 'Sydney Lodge' in Hampshire. As noted, many members of the Yorke family, following their interest in naval affairs, had lived there and had been baptised and were buried in St Andrew's Church there.

In the 12th century there was a priory on the ground where St Andrew's church was built three centuries later. It was situated, just outside the village of Hamble, on the road which runs from there to Hound, a neighbouring parish.

In the church are stained glass windows which commemorate various members of the Yorke family and, in addition, there are several wall plaques which do the same. The latest recorded was in 1958, illustrating the family's lengthy involvement with Hamble and its church.

In the 20th Century, the area surrounding the village of Hamble changed dramatically. Although the village has retained much of its earlier character with its cottages, inns and small shops situated around the Quay, the area outside changed through the development of the aircraft industry which started in 1916 when A V Roe purchased land at Hamble.

The work of Avro and, subsequently, several different companies formed through amalgamations or take-overs continued for forty years, bringing hundreds of people to the area, building houses and shops as well as developing numerous factory buildings. Some of the companies involved were British Marine Aircraft, Folland Aircraft Ltd., and Hawker Siddeley Aviation. (see link with Tommy Sopwith – Childwickbury).

Today the industrial site outside of Hamble village is owned by G E Aviation (General Electric) and their many buildings have completely surrounded Sydney Lodge. The lodge is uninhabited, cannot be pulled down as it is a listed building, and nobody from the 'outside world' is allowed on the site.

The stable block, built on land purchased by Lady Agneta on her arrival at Hamble, and situated closer to the Solent than 'Sydney Lodge', has now been converted into offices, a telephone exchange and directors' accommodation. The block can be seen from a coastal path.

8

Family Connections of Frederic J Hall

As noted in 'Northaw Place', Frederic Hall was the first member of the Hall Family to live in Northaw.

He was the second of the three sons of Thomas Grainger Hall and Eliza Kitson, and was born in 'Wenlock' a large house in Torquay on 5th August 1846.

In 1851 when Frederic was four years old, he was recorded on the census, living with his family in Chester Square, Belgravia, in London. As a young man, he was sent to Shrewsbury School as a boarder, as were his brothers. All of the Hall boys played in the School's Cricket 1st XI. From Shrewsbury, he gained a Scholarship and went up to Clare College, Cambridge, where he obtained a BA in 1869.

In that year, at the age of 23, he became an Assistant Master at Haileybury College in Hertfordshire. He was ordained in 1871 and became a priest the following year. At this time he gained his MA.

In the Summer of 1881, after 12 years, Frederic left his post at Haileybury. His father died on 26th August of that year and Frederic and his brother George would have travelled to Paignton, both for the funeral and as executors of their father's will.

While there, Frederic would have been in close contact with the Reverend Poland in order to organise his father's funeral at the Parish Church. He formed a close relationship with Elizabeth, the eldest daughter of Frederick and Mary Poland, and married her two years later (see Poland Family).

In the same year that he married, Frederic acquired a school in 'Wymondley House', close to Hitchin.

'Wymondley House' was built in 1724 by John Pym. It had a Georgian façade and contained more than forty rooms. Members of the Pym family lived in the house until it was sold in 1799. For some years after, it was used as a non-conformist Theological College. In

1834 the house became a private boarding school for boys, kept by the Reverend J. J. Tuck MA, a schoolmaster and clerk in holy orders. In 1871 there were sixteen pupils boarding there, according to the census for that year.

When Reverend Tuck retired from teaching, the school was taken over by Frederic and he remained there for eight years.

During their time at Wymondley, Frederic and Elizabeth had four daughters and a son. Their eldest daughter, Margaret, was born there in 1884 but the other children were all born in Paignton. Clearly, after the birth of her first child in Hertfordshire, Elizabeth decided to return to her mother's care, where, perhaps, the conditions were more favourable than in her husband's boarding school.

A daughter, Elizabeth, was born two years after Margaret and then there was great excitement when, in 1887, their mother gave birth to 'identical' twins, Georgina and Dorothy. One of the pupils of the school couldn't wait to inform his parents that 'Old Hall', as he was known, had become the father of twins. Neither 'Old Hall' nor the pupil, aged 11, had any idea that, one day, one of those twins would marry that pupil.

Frederick Grainger Hall was born at the end of 1890 and was the first of Frederic and Elizabeth's sons.

In 1891 there were twenty eight boarders, aged between fifteen and nine years of age, who came from all over England and Ireland, India and Ceylon. The latter were British subjects. One notable name recorded was that of Thomas S. Attlee from Putney, the son of Henry and Ellen Attlee, the close friends of Frederic's father. At this time the Attlee's eldest son, Robert, was an undergraduate at Oxford and their son, Clement was eight years old, having been born in January 1883.

As well as running the school, Frederic was also the Vicar of Little Wymondley from 1890 until 1891.

In 1891 he decided to leave Wymondley and move to Northaw. He bought 'Northaw Place', opening it as a Preparatory School for Boys. Frederick Poland, his brother-in-law, who had assisted him at Wymondley joined him at Northaw, as did a number of his former pupils, including Thomas Attlee. Mrs Ross, the School Matron who came from Scotland, went to Northaw as well. She was forty two at this time.

The house was enlarged from its two storeys with a hipped gable, flat roof and cupola, to a three storey building. Several other building changes were made. A large room, used as an assembly hall, was built with dormitories above. This was joined to the old part by a long narrow glass-roofed passage. A back staircase, a dining room and a kitchen were added. The family lived in the old part of the house, with the servants. The third floor had seven bedrooms.

There was also a walled garden with a swimming pool, as well as a Cricket ground placed half way up the parkland.

In the Summer of 1892 Clement Attlee, then nine, joined his brother, Thomas, at the school. Previously he had been taught at home by his mother in a strong Church of England family environment.

In his autobiography, 'As It Happened', Attlee described his education at Northaw in some detail. No doubt, his time there made a lasting and deep impression upon the young boy. There were about forty boarders at the school. Not surprisingly, he described Hall as a mathematician, obviously following in his father's footsteps. Apparently Poland was no scholar and the other assistants, who came from time to time, had not been trained to teach and were not qualified to give other than fairly elementary education.

Such education took place in the large room when various 'sets' were formed at tables and pupils were called out to stand in line to receive oral instruction in Latin.

A good deal of time was devoted to studying the Bible, particularly the Old Testament, and pupils left with a sound knowledge of the Kings of Israel and Judah. The history of the Jews was taught straight through from Joshua and Judges to Ezra and Nehemiah. Attlee felt that 'An incredible amount of time was wasted in acquiring useless knowledge. There was no exegesis at this time. It was all holy writ'.

'History and Geography were taught in the usual manner of the time, a list of facts, and the teaching of Classics was thoroughly bad, so that those who went from Northaw struggled to compete with other pupils who had received a satisfactory education in this field in their early years'.

The care taken of the boys was immense and the ambience of the place was delightful. Mrs Hall was an extremely competent person ably assisted by 'an old Scots person', Mrs Ross, who was the matron. The food was excellent, the grounds were extensive and beautiful and Attlee spent very happy times there. He wrote of cosy evenings in the gas-lit schoolroom, Mrs Hall at the piano in the beautiful drawing room, and skating on the pond in the hard winter of 1895.

He states that the real 'religion' of Hall and Poland was cricket. Their 'Holy of Holies' was the Pavilion at Lords! Following his success in playing cricket at Shrewsbury and his obvious love of the game, every afternoon throughout the summer, cricket was played on a very reasonable pitch. The boys invented games of cricket, played on paper, during the evenings. Although Attlee was never much use as a batsman or bowler, he did aspire to being a good fielder.

In the winter, rugger was the game and Hall took an active part until he was well over fifty.

Attlee wrote 'Northaw sent out few scholars but plenty of good professional, gentlemanly cricketers!'

Nevertheless, in 1896, Attlee went on to Haileybury and to Oxford, and several others who attended Northaw went on to highly successful careers. Hilton Young became a Minister in Ramsay Macdonald's government, William Jowitt was a Lord Chancellor and a distinguished lawyer and then there was Lord David Cecil. Surely Frederic Hall had achieved something!

At this time, 1890, Frederic's son, John Buller Edward Hall was born. The Census for 1901 records the Reverend Hall, aged fifty four, and his wife, Elizabeth, forty six, with four daughters and two sons at 'Northaw Place'.

As a child, one of the twins, Dorothy, was frequently unwell, suffering from asthma. A German governess was appointed to look after the children. This was beneficial to all of the children as they were able to travel to Germany and it was here that their real musical abilities were discovered.

During 'term time' at Northaw, as the children grew up, they mixed with the pupils and gave their mother assistance in looking after the sixty or so pupils. In the school holidays, there were dances, parties and other social events in the house and grounds.

Frederic organised frequent cricket matches between the boys, the 'old boys' and the villagers. The 'old boys' were not just those from Northaw but from Wymondley as well. One of those was the boy who was so excited when the twins were born. He was Philip Devitt. Philip became a frequent visitor to Northaw and a great friend of the Hall family.

In 1911 the Inland Revenue Survey assessed the value of the property in Northaw. Frederic owned fifty one acres of parkland. The house, 'Northaw Place', and various school buildings, the lodge and the garden cottage were valued at £9,750. 'St Just' was valued at £800 and 'Northacre' at £2,500.

The Halls second daughter, Elizabeth, known as 'Elsie', married Hugh William Priestley, a Stockbroker, on January 26th 1911(see Priestley file).

The Hall family remained at 'Northaw Place' until Frederic decided to retire from his teaching in 1912 when he was sixty six. He left Northaw in the hands of Cecil Esdaile Winter and the Reverend Percy Cyril Underhill and the school continued without him.

He moved from Hertfordshire and became the Vicar of Shirburn in Oxfordshire and was there for ten years. He was also the Rural Dean of Aston from 1915 until 1922.

On some occasions, the Vicar of Shirburn and his family lived in The Rectory in nearby Pyrton, the 'pear tree place', while the Vicar of Pyrton lived in the Vicarage. At other times the living was held jointly. When the Hall Family were in this area they lived in the Vicarage at Pyrton.

Shirburn Church, next to Shirburn Castle, dates from the 13th century although much alteration and restoration took place in the

19th century. Since that time, the church has gradually fallen into a state of disrepair. For a long time, repairs to the church were paid for by the successive Earls of Macclesfield who owned the neighbouring castle and surrounding estate from 1732. Since the Second World War, with fewer people being employed on the estate and ever-increasing building costs, the need for repairs escalated until it was decided to declare the church redundant. No longer is the church used and it has been placed in the hands of the Church Conservation Trust.

The quadrangular castle was a new design of the 14th century. For the first time a castle managed to combine both its domestic and military roles in one building. It comprised ranges of buildings around a square courtyard defended by walls and corner towers and had a moat and drawbridge. It was similar to the Welsh castles of Harlech and Caernarfon.

The castle had many owners until an 18th century lawyer, Thomas Parker, called 'silver-tongued Parker', acquired the estate. He became Lord Chancellor and the Earl of Macclesfield under King George I. However, he was impeached for corruption, retiring to Shirburn in disgrace. He died there in 1732 but his descendants still live there.

For much of the 18th Century the vicars of Shirburn were virtually personal chaplains to the Macclesfields and some even lived in the castle. Frederick Hall and his family were certainly very involved with the Macclesfield family as events showed.

During much of their time in Shirburn, the First World War was a dominant factor in their lives. There is no doubt that Northaw was greatly missed by all of the family.

Perhaps the greatest sadness to the family during the war was the death of Frederic's elder son, Edward Grainger Hall. He had joined the Army and had become a captain of 13th Battalion of the Cheshire Regiment.

On 6th July 1916 the Battalion occupied trenches in the village of La Boiselle. On that day the casualties had been relatively small. A Second Lieutenant, a CSM, Sergeants and four other ranks were wounded.

On Friday 7th at 8.05 a.m. the Battalion 'went over the parapet'. After suffering severe casualties, their objective was reached and the battalion consolidated. A number of prisoners and war material fell into their hands but the casualties were very heavy. Eighteen officers, including Captain Edward Grainger Hall, aged twenty five, and two hundred and forty three other ranks were killed on that morning. Edward is remembered in the Serre Road Cemetry in that area of France together with many of the thousands of other men whose lives were lost in the Battle of The Somme.

Margaret volunteered to be a nurse at the beginning of the war. She was thirty and she trained in Beaconsfield Memorial Hospital for three months before going to France to work with the French Red Cross in the Military Hospital in Wimereux in 1915. This was followed by her working in the London General Hospital in Denmark Hill before returning to France for another year. In the last months of the war she was in the London General Hospital in Chelsea. She was awarded a Scarlet Efficiency Stripe in 1917.

Dorothy, then 26, also volunteered and trained at the Cottage Hospital in High Wycombe for four months before transferring as a nurse to different BEF Hospitals in France from June, 1915 to 1918, working and living in tents. It was this experience that was to lead to her suffering from severe arthritis in her later life.

Georgina was an Ambulance Driver from May 1918 with the French Red Cross. She undertook several very dangerous missions that others refused and was commended for her bravery. Driving her ambulance, she escaped, after the fall of Paris, through St Nazaire.

While at the Vicarage, Elizabeth, in her sixties, an excellent cook and housekeeper, kept several cows that she milked herself to provide butter and cream. She was assisted in this by her daughters who took it in turns to be with their parents as often as possible.

At about the time of the Armistice, late in 1918, Dorothy and Philip Devitt were engaged to be married. The wedding was fixed for 22nd February 1919. (see Devitt file)

The Hall's eldest daughter, Margaret, married Harold Walter Lake in 1921 in St George's Church in Hanover Square, London (see Lake Family).

The Halls left Shirburn in 1922 and returned to Northaw where they lived in 'St Just' for the rest of their days. At this time Edith Poland moved to a cottage close by in Northaw, 'St Erth', named after her mother's village near St Ives in Cornwall. She remained there until she died at the age of eighty six in 1948. She was buried at Northaw on 17th March of that year.

In 1922 Mr Esdaile Winter was running the school and remained there until its closure in 1928, although the school still belonged to Frederic Hall.

At this time he transferred the ownership of 'Northaw Place' jointly to his four daughters and, at the same time, made his will at St Just when no mention was made of 'Northaw Place'. Codicils were added to the will in 1935.

At the age of ninety, Frederic died at St Just in 1936 and was buried in Northaw on 19th September, just before the start of the Second World War. He left an estate with a gross value of nearly £16,000. His grave adjoins that of Hugh Priestley.

Frederic's younger son, John Buller Edward Hall, born in 1895 was baptised in Northaw Church on 4th August. He joined the Royal Navy as a young man. He worked his way through the ranks and was a Lieutenant Commander on HMS Coventry in 1926 when he was thirty and was in charge of physical and recreational training. He was on the Queen Elizabeth in 1929 and he became a commander in 1930. He was in the crew of HMS Wellington in 1938.

At the start of World War Two he was made captain of HMS Princess Victoria, a mine-laying ship based at Immingham, off the Humber estuary. On 18th May 1940, the ship was returning home after two days of mine laying in the North Sea when there was an enormous explosion. Twelve of the seventeen officers and ratings on the bridge were flung into the sea and drowned and there were thirty four casualties altogether. There was an official enquiry to attempt to establish the cause of the explosion and the loss of so many lives but the findings were inconclusive.

Elizabeth had lost her second son at the age of forty four and Jean had lost her husband, 'Jack', as he was known. He is remembered on the Chatham Naval Memorial.

During the Second World War, 'St Just' was occupied by other members of the Priestley family on a temporary basis. Elizabeth, with a nurse to care for her, returned to 'St Just' soon after peace was announced. Plans to sell 'Northaw Place' for development were firmly resisted.

Elizabeth remained at 'St Just' until, at the age of 94, she died in 1947 and was buried in Northaw on 6th December in the grave with her husband Frederic. She left 'St Just' to Jean Hall, her son John's widow, and their two daughters, Joanna and Penny. She also left Spinney Cottage, sometimes called 'Red Cottage', next to St Just, to her unmarried daughter Georgina. However Jean decided not to live there. The four Hall daughters were then the owners of 'Northaw Place'.

Dorothy's twin sister, 'Georgie', did not marry. She continued to serve her country during the Second World War. She was the commandant of 44th (Herts) VAD and played a significant part in the Girl Guide Movement. She remained at her cottage until her death in August 1979 when she was buried on 20th August in the family grave. She was ninety two.

The Poland Family –
Paignton in Devon and Northaw

The vicar of St John's Church in Paignton, the Reverend Frederick William Poland, born in Islington in 1827, was the fourth son of Sir William Henry Poland. He went to Emmanuel College, Cambridge in 1845 and graduated in 1849 when he was made a Deacon in Exeter. He became a Priest the following year and gained an MA in 1852.

While he was a Curate in St Ives in Cornwall he met his future wife, Mary, the daughter of William Hichens, an Attorney at Law of St Ives. They were married in April 1852.

Subsequently he became a curate in two other areas in Cornwall before moving to London for a short period of time.

Frederick and Mary had two sons and four daughters. Their eldest daughters, Elizabeth and Mary, and their son, William, were born in Cornwall.

The 1861 census recorded the family in Hammersmith where Frederick was the curate of St Stephen's Church. Their son was shown as being born in Shepherds Bush, London the year before.

Another daughter, Edith, was born in London in 1862, the year before Frederick became the Rural Dean of Ippleden on the outskirts of Torquay.

He became vicar of Paignton with Marldon in Devon in 1871 and lived in the Vicarage there for thirty years.

It was at this time that his family became associated with Thomas Grainger Hall and his family. It was in 1881 when Thomas died that the Poland family became more closely involved with Frederic Hall and his brothers and it was a very short time after this that Frederic married Elizabeth Poland, their eldest daughter.

The Poland's son, William Henry, also became a clergyman following his studies at Cambridge. He was made a deacon in 1880 and was the curate of Ottery St Mary Church in Devon before becoming the vicar of Linkinhorne, in the Diocese of Truro, where he remained for eight years, living in the village of Callington.

He married Laura, another member of the Hichens family in 1886 at Lexden in Essex and, in 1893, he and Laura were to make another Hertfordshire connection. William became Rector of Shephall, a part of Stevenage.

In 1901, the census recorded William and Laura, living in Shephall Rectory. They had a son Richard Hichens Poland, aged 1, who was born in Datchworth, Herts and a daughter, Cicely Mabel Poland, 2, born in Shephall, a short distance away.

With them was Frederick W Poland, 41, Henry's brother and Frederic Hall's brother-in-law, shown as a clergyman in the Church of England.

Frederick William, obtained a BA degree while at Trinity College Cambridge in 1882. He became a deacon in 1884 and a priest in

1887. He worked in the Church in Stevenage in the Diocese of St Albans from 1884 until 1892.

The 1891 Census described him still as a curate in Stevenage but also as an assistant in Frederic Hall's preparatory School in Wymondley and when the Hall Family moved to Northaw, Frederick went with them.

Ten years later, he was not working at 'Northaw Place' but remained a curate in Stevenage. A short while after this he made the decision to move to Canada. He worked there, in the Diocese of Montreal, until he retired in 1933 when he was 73 years old.

The Reverend Frederick William Poland MA Snr. retired from his position as Vicar of Paignton in 1892 and he and Mary, his wife, and his daughter, Edith, lived in 'Northacre', a large house in the grounds of 'Northaw Place' built for him by his son-in-law on the large estate that he had purchased. Mary died there in November, 1893 and was buried in Northaw on 9th November when the Reverend Baron Hitchens officiated. At the present time, 2010, extensive restoration is being carried out on the property.

Frederick Poland died in 'Northacre' at the age of 77. He was buried in Northaw on 10th December. On his death in 1903, his daughter, Edith, moved into the smaller house, 'St Just', also in the grounds of 'Northaw Place'.

Margaret Hall and Harold Lake

Margaret, the eldest daughter of Frederic and Elizabeth Hall, married Harold Walter Lake at Christ Church, Broadway, in Westminster, London, on 28th April, 1921.

During his life, Harold Lake was closely linked to the Greene King Brewery in Bury St Edmund's and, to understand something of this, it is necessary to look briefly at the development of this brewery and the people who were involved.

The Greene Family – Bury St Edmunds in Suffolk

Benjamin Greene, born in 1780, was the youngest of thirteen children who survived from the two marriages of his father. He followed in his father's footsteps in becoming a draper in Bedfordshire.

When Benjamin was 22 months old his father died. The Greene family were Dissenters and gained much support from their religious communities. As he grew up, Benjamin's faith became extremely important to him. He was given a sound education and, through his family's connections at their chapel, he was given the opportunity to become an apprentice in Samuel Whitbread's brewery in London.

After serving nine years there, Benjamin moved to Bury where John Clark owned a brewery in Guildhall. Benjamin signed a three year agreement to work with him. There were connections between the Clark and Greene families, both having roots in Bedfordshire.

In 1803, Benjamin married Mary Maling, the daughter of a yarn merchant of Bury. She died shortly after the marriage and a year later, in 1805, Benjamin married Catherine Smith, the daughter of the minister of the Howard Chapel in Bedford where the Greene family were members. This marriage produced seven sons and six daughters, two sons dying in infancy.

The Greene/Clark partnership did not succeed and in 1805 Benjamin agreed to form another partnership with William Buck, a prosperous yarn maker, who decided, because of the decline in his trade, to change direction and take over the brewery of the Wright family.

Throughout the 18th Century, there had been a brewery in Westgate Street, Bury, owned by successive generations of the Wright Family. They became very prosperous from brewing and farming which were always closely linked. However, it was decided to sell the brewery in 1798. There was no quick sale but, finally in the winter of 1805, it was purchased by Benjamin Greene and William Buck. Both William and Benjamin were members of the Independent Chapel in Whiting Street and were highly regarded in Bury.

It was this William Buck whose daughter, Catherine, a vivacious and talented girl, had married William Clarkson in 1794.

The Greene/Buck brewery was successful and, after William Buck died in 1819, Benjamin continued to run the business. At the same time as managing the brewery, he sought to widen his interests.

He acquired the 'Bury and Suffolk Herald', a provincial newspaper, in 1828. Articles appearing in the paper were directly opposed to the views of Thomas Clarkson on the subject of slavery. This resulted in an exchange of correspondence between Greene and Clarkson and letters appeared in the Herald for some months. Benjamin's opposition to the anti-slavery legislation caused considerable public reaction and he faced three libel cases. This reaction caused him to leave Bury and move to London, leaving the everyday running of the brewery in the hands of his son, Edward.

He became much more involved in the family's business ventures in London, the West Indies and Mauritius. He became a planter on a considerable scale in St Kitts, one of the most fertile islands of the West Indies, as well as managing large estates there for family friends.

In 1836 in Mincing Lane, London, he founded a sugar importing and shipowning firm. He died, aged 80, in Russell Square in November 1860 and was buried in Highgate Cemetery.

His eldest son, Benjamin Buck Greene, followed in his footsteps in the West Indies before becoming highly successful as a London Banker and a Governor of the Bank of England.

In 1901 the Census recorded him as a retired merchant, aged ninety two and widowed, living in Midgham House, near Newbury. With him were his two unmarried daughters, aged sixty two and fifty five, both born in Bloomsbury, London. They employed a cook, a footman and a butler, with a lady's maid and four other maids. In addition, living in accommodation in the stable yard, were three coachmen and a groom and their families.

Benjamin Buck Greene's brother, John, a JP and twice Mayor of Bury worked as a solicitor in the town.

Eventually their father, Benjamin, left his West Indian property to be divided among his numerous grandchildren.

When Edward, his third son came of age in 1836, Benjamin left the brewery entirely in his hands.

Edward, like all of his brothers, was educated at Bury Grammar School and entered the family brewery when he was thirteen. He had no experience elsewhere. In spite of this, he was instrumental in transforming the small country brewery into one of regional significance.

In 1840 he married Emily, the fourth daughter of the Reverend Henry Yeats Smithies and his wife, Isabella, of Huntingdon. Emily was born in 1820 in Stanground on the outskirts of Peterborough. She died at the age of twenty eight, having had five children. Edward was left to bring up these children, all under the age of seven. Outside of his commitment to the brewery, he had always devoted his time to his family and he took no part in the social activities in and around Bury. He employed a governess to help in the care of his children and it was not until twenty two years later that he married again.

In 1851, the census recorded him with five children and four servants as well as employing eighteen men and three boys. Ten years later he had increased his business tenfold since taking over and was employing forty five men and three boys. He made extensions and alterations to the brewery, bringing in more modern appliances and additional equipment.

His hard work and enterprise for nearly thirty years, when he was in constant daily attention at the brewery in Westgate Street, had to change in 1865 when he became a Conservative MP for Bury St Edmunds, which he represented for twenty years. He left Westgate Street and rented the estate of 'Ixworth Abbey', about six miles from Bury, where he farmed extensively.

In 1870 he married again. His wife, Caroline, was the widow of a rear-admiral and baronet, Sir William Hoste, who had rented 'Westgate House' from Edward in 1865. Three years later the admiral died. His widow remained in Bury and saw a good deal of her landlord whom she married two years later.

Caroline Dorothea was born in 1827 in London, the daughter

of Charles Prideaux-Brune and Frances Glyn. She was twelve years younger than Edward. Her family had a sound social standing in London and in the West Country and, no doubt, she would have enhanced Edward's position amongst the Suffolk gentry, especially by keeping her name, Lady Hoste. She had two children before her marriage to Edward and another afterwards in 1872.

In 1871, Edward Greene began purchasing public houses throughout West Suffolk. This took place as a result of the competition he faced from a neighbouring brewery owned by the King family. Edward was forced to move from a 'free trade' situation into selling through his own public houses. In the same way, Fred King was expanding in order to compete.

In 1874 Edward purchased an entire estate known as 'Nether Hall', near Thurston and due east of Bury. This included the 'Manor House' which was a large brick-built mansion in the Queen Anne style and situated in extensive grounds and woodland areas. Restoration took place during the following year and the property was enlarged.

In the space of ten years Edward Greene and Fred King had become two of the largest property owners in the country. Greene had an eight hundred and fifty acre estate, property in Bury and over ninety public houses. The two men realised that the future lay in the amalgamation of their companies, rather than competing against each other. In 1877 this amalgamation took place and Green King Ltd became one of the largest country brewers in England.

The 1891 census recorded Edward, aged seventy five, living at 'Nether Hall' as a brewer and a Member of Parliament. With him was his wife, Caroline, then sixty three, and their unmarried daughter, Ethel, aged nineteen. There were eleven servants living in the 'Hall'; as well as housekeeper, two lady's maids, a butler, two footmen, a cook and four maids. Living in adjoining cottages were the coachman/groom with his wife and family and the gardener with his wife and family.

After entering Parliament, Edward left the day to day running of the brewery to this son, (Edward) Walter Greene, and later to his nephew, Edward William Lake.

Walter had been taken into the firm as a partner in 1862 at the age of twenty. His education at Bury Grammar School, where his father and uncles had studied, was cut short after only a term when his father decided it was not of the standard required. Walter was sent to join Dr Arnold at Rugby. He did not achieve any great academic success in spite of the change and always stated that he had little time for books. He was, however, well-mannered and conscientious and had acquired many social acquaintances. He studied Languages in Paris, travelled through Europe and completed his training for working in the family brewery at Tamplin's brewery in Brighton.

Walter showed no real interest in, or aptitude for, running the brewery. He was extremely sociable, an excellent sportsman, a keen yachtsman and had a great passion for horse riding and hunting which he had inherited from his father. Although, his father believed, his social activities gave the family an increased presence in the county, the time expended on such activities was not benefiting the management of the brewery or increasing its development.

Nevertheless Walter played some part in ensuring that the development of the brewery was maintained. He became a Justice of the Peace and, at the age of thirty nine, was recorded on the 1881 census as living in 'Westgate House', next to the brewery, with his wife, their four daughters and a son of two months. He employed a governess, a footman, a butler, a nurse, a cook and four maids. He was said to be employing eighty five men in the brewery at that time.

On the death of his father in 1891, Walter returned to 'Nether Hall' and enlarged and modernised it. He lived there for only a small part of each year as he followed the lifestyle of the super rich of the time. From March to April he would travel to the Continent, usually Monte Carlo. In June he would take an active part in Cowes week. The following month would see him in Scotland for grouse shooting and deer stalking. In September, he would return to 'Nether Hall' for partridge shooting and, during the winter months, he would go to Newmarket for racing and make trips to London, where he had an apartment in Albermarle Street. However, he did find time to take an active part in church life in Suffolk at Thurston Church, where he was a patron.

In 1897 he became a High Sheriff of the County and in 1900 he received the Baronetcy which had been promised to his father before he died. He was elected as a Conservative Member of Parliament from 1900 until 1905. When he died in 1920, 'Nether Hall' was sold. His sons, Raymond and Edward, both became Chairmen and Directors of Greene King until the middle of the 20th Century.

Although Walter had shown some concern for the brewery and had ensured a certain degree of stability, it was Edward Lake who was the inspiration of the development that was to take place.

The Lake Family & Greene King in Suffolk

The success of the Bury brewery itself was really the result of the hard work of Edward Lake. In 1869, Edward Greene had taken his nephew, Edward Lake, into the firm.

Edward William Lake was the youngest of the eight children of Henry Lake, a solicitor, and his wife, Mary, a sister of Edward Greene and daughter of Benjamin Greene. Henry Lake and Mary Greene married in Bury in 1836 before moving to London. Henry had offices in Lincoln's Inn, London, and bought a house in The Grove at Highgate in North London where Edward was born.

Their house, 'No.1 The Grove' was one of three pairs of early semi-detached houses built by William Blake in this delightful, tree-lined, road situated just off Highgate Village. Nos. 1 and 2 were converted to a single residence in 1931, before the Lake family arrived. About the same time, No 3 underwent considerable alteration. It was at this time that the property was purchased by Mr J B Priestley, the author and playwright, who sold it in 1948. Prior to this, the property was owned by Dr Gillman who moved there from South Grove at the end of 1923 (see Clarkson file). No. 1/2 was purchased in 1959 by the internationally famous violinist, Yehudi Menuhin, before he opened the Menuhin School in Surrey in 1963.

When Henry Lake died, Edward Greene agreed to help his widowed sister, Mary, by training her youngest son, Edward, in the brewery in Bury, even though his elder brothers had followed their father and become solicitors.

The 1861 Census recorded Edward Lake, aged 9, as a boarder in a private school in Montpelier Crescent in Brighton. The school was organised in seven joined houses and there were thirty pupils in residence, coming from areas all over the country. In addition to several teachers there was a large number of domestic staff including one servant who was born in Cheshunt, Hertfordshire!

Several members of the Lake family lived in Brighton and this may have had something to do with the choice of a school in this town for Edward.

Ten years later Edward was established in the brewery business and in 1875 he was made a partner in the brewery.

In August 1877, he married Blanche Frampton Dewe at St Peter's Church in Brighton. Blanche was the daughter of William Dewe, a prosperous farmer of seven hundred acres of land in Sapperton, Gloucestershire.

Blanche's mother, Mary, died in 1871 and her father married again in 1873. His wife, Louisa, was six years older than he and was born in Guernsey in the Channel Islands. The family, including Blanche, moved to Brighton when her father retired from farming.

By 1889 Edward was established as a director of Greene King. In that year, he and the managing director, Frederick William King, bought Rayment's brewery at Furneaux Pelham in Hertfordshire which they ran as an independent undertaking. Attached to this was 'Lodge Farm', having an area of three hundred and fifty acres, which was worked as a joint project. Members of the Lake family were involved in the management until 1967.

Edward and Blanche had seven daughters and six sons while living in Bury. After preparatory schooling in Bury, the boys were sent to Uppingham School in Rutland.

Their sons had distinguished military careers during the First World War. On their return, four of them were decorated together by

King George V.

Their eldest son, Edward Lancelot Dewe Lake, was born in 1881, a twin brother of Muriel Dewe Lake. After his education at Uppingham, he trained at Brakspear's brewery at Henley-on-Thames and served for three years in the First World War when he became a major. In 1919, at the age of thirty-eight, he was appointed managing director of Greene King and worked unceasingly for the company, often in adverse circumstances, until his death in 1946. He was chairman of the Brewers' Society from 1934 to 1936 and was nine times mayor of Bury as well as being a JP. The undoubted success of Greene King in the 21st Century owes much to the earlier work of Edward and his father. This success has been well-documented in Richard G Wilson's 'Greene King'. Their houses and products are clearly visible for all to see today.

A younger son, Harold Walter Lake, was born in 1882, a year after Edward and Muriel. After his education at Uppingham, Harold went up to Oriel College, Oxford, where he gained an Honours Degree in Law in 1905.

He was recorded on the 1911 Census as a boarder in the house of a domestic gardener living in Lyndale Hill, Brow Road, Esher. Harold's two younger sisters, Aileen and Doreen, both still at school, were visiting him at the time of the census. Aileen married in 1922 and her son, Martin Dewe Corke, born the following year, became a director of Greene King in 1953 and the Managing Director from 1983.

Harold practised in Lincoln's Inn as a solicitor until 1912 when he went to Rayment's brewery. He served in the First World War when he was a lieutenant in the Coldstream Guards. He was awarded a Military Cross in 1919.

Harold's younger brother, Alan, born in 1887, became the managing director of Rayment's, the brewery at Pelham Furneaux from 1912 until 1930, as well as farming the three hundred and fifty acres that adjoined the brewery. Harold spent some time there living at the farm as well as working at the brewery. On Alan's death, the brewery was merged with Greene King. Until 1937 it was managed by a nephew

Northaw Place

Northaw Place Stable Block

View of Northaw Place

Wenlock in Torquay

Wymondley House near Hitchin

Haileybury College in Hertford

The Vicarage at Pyrton

Shirburn Church, Oxford

Shirburn Church and Castle

St. Just in Northaw

of Edward Lake Snr., a Vice Admiral W J C Lake CBE and then Alan's younger brother, Henry Neville Lake, who was a Captain in the Royal Navy. He had been awarded a DSO and DSC and became the Managing Director from 1938 until 1967.

The Brothers of Edward Greene –
West Indies, Bedford and Cambridge

Apart from the Lake Family linking with the Hall Family in Hertfordshire, the Greene Family also had connections with Hertfordshire.

Edward Greene of Nether Hall, had two younger brothers, (Henry) Charles born in 1821 and William in 1824. Both of the boys were educated at Bury School and, at an early age were sent to the West Indies by Benjamin, their father, to manage the family estates, following their older brother Benjamin Buck Greene.

Charles was sixteen when he arrived there and was immediately put in charge of the family affairs. He succeeded in fulfilling his father's wishes and was a good manager. However, he also enjoyed 'the good life' in the warm sunshine in a land of many temptations. He died, in 1840, still under nineteen, after four days of yellow fever, having, according to legend, fathered a large number of illegitimate children.

William, aged fourteen, arrived out there in 1839, having spent a year in his father's office in Bury. He helped Charles, enjoying his time there. He remained there for a short time after his brother's death in 1840. He returned to Bury, after his contracting yellow fever himself. His report to his father on the state of affairs in St Kitts was not found to be very satisfactory. Nevertheless he was allowed to return to St Kitts in 1843. He was totally unsuited to what was required of him in terms of management and the business was declining, He was not an administrator or a businessman in any respect. He was a nervous and highly-strung young man and so he returned to Bury.

In 1854, William married Charlotte Smith who was born in Lincolnshire in 1831. She was the daughter of a coastal shipping master. She was a very sensible woman who was able to provide great comfort for her children in a very unsettled family life and she and William had a good marriage, she giving him every support that was possible. They had nine children.

William was a dreamer who loved reading but sadly his education had been limited and he was unable to take full advantage of his delight in literature. He was given further work to undertake but proved to be no more successful.

The 1871 Census recorded Charlotte, aged twenty nine, as a farmer of one hundred and seventy acres, employing seven men and three boys. Four of her children, whose ages ranged from five years to six months, were with her at the farm in Takeley, Essex. Her husband, William, was not there at the time of the census but there was a nursemaid, as well as a housemaid, a cook and a page boy living with the family.

The farm was not a success and the family moved to Henley on Thames in Oxfordshire where sons, Charles and Edward, were born. The family moved to Granchester in Cambridge and another four children were born. Finally they settled in Bedford.

The Greene family had provided William with an income and he decided to move to Bedford in order to send his sons to a good school that was not too costly. The family paid for a large house with a large garden that he occupied with his large family.

While there he endeavoured to run a peat company but took no real interest in this venture. He took long walks, with a book in his pocket, went missing for long periods and spent his nights in a hut on the black peat bogs of the area. Family life was not for him and, when he was at home, he spent his time in a study reading and writing of the places he longed to visit.

The 1881 Census recorded the family living at their large house, 44 Potter Street in Bedford St Mary. William was fifty six and Charlotte was forty nine. At this time their daughter Florence was twenty five, Alice was twenty three and Charlotte twenty. Charles Henry was sixteen, Edward fourteen, Frederick thirteen, Benjamin twelve, and Helen ten. They had two servants living in the household. Their eldest son, William Graham Greene, was not with them, as he was twenty four and being educated elsewhere.

Suddenly in May of 1881, in a state of acute depression, following his young business partner's suicide, William decided to return to St Kitts. This was an attempt to recapture the earlier times that he had enjoyed there as a youth and satisfy his frustrated romantic nature. He contracted fever, once again, and died within days. The family arranged for him to be buried next to his brother, Charles.

Ten years later William's family were living in Haslingfield Road in Harston, in the south of Cambridgeshire where they were staying in the house of Arthur Tuck, a farmer. The census at this time shows Charlotte 'living on her own means' with her sons, William Graham Greene, by this time, a Private Secretary in the Admiralty, and Edward Greene, 24, a merchant working in Brazil. Their elder sister, Florence, who was then Mrs Philips, was staying with them. Shortly after this Charlotte and her son, William, purchased "Harston House", a short distance away.

In spite of the inability of Charlotte's husband, William, to achieve the expectations of his father, he and his wife, who had never met the family's expectations for William, produced children that any grandfather would have admired immensely. Benjamin Greene, of course, was not alive to see them achieve their undoubted, wide-ranging success.

The Sons of William Greene in Hertfordshire

William, the eldest son of William and Charlotte Greene, born in 1857, was educated at Cheltenham College and in Germany before working for four years in the family brewery in Bury.

After this work experience, he took up posts in surveying and engineering before joining the Civil Service where he had an outstanding career. In 1907 he became Assistant Secretary of the Admiralty. Four years later he was made a KCB and became Permanent Secretary. In 1914, at the outbreak of hostilities, Winston Churchill made him one of his staff group who made decisions on important matters relating to the war.

At this time William had a flat close to Grosvenor Square, in London. He remained in his post in the Admiralty until 1917 and became Permanent Secretary in the Ministry of Munitions from then until 1920. He was said to be one of the ablest civil servants of his generation.

He retired to spend most of his time at Harston, where he became fully occupied in local activities. He was a JP and a County Councillor for Cambridge. He died on 10th September, 1950 at his house. There is a memorial plaque in the parish church which states that he was buried at sea. The clergyman, Canon Baldwin, who held the living at Harston, was a frequent visitor of the Greene's in Berkhamsted.

Charles Henry Greene

William's younger brother, Charles Henry Greene, went up, as an Exhibitioner, to Wadham College in Oxford before deciding to become a schoolmaster. Undoubtedly his decision was influenced by a number of different factors.

In 1876, when he was eleven, his cousin Julia, born in 1846, the daughter of Edward Greene of 'Nether Hall', married The Reverend Dr Thomas Charles Fry. This family connection changed the course of Charles's life.

Like Charles, Thomas Fry, the son of a solicitor in Bedford, was a former pupil of Bedford Grammar School. In 1864, he won an open scholarship to Pembroke College, Cambridge. He went on to teach at Durham School before moving to Cheltenham College and, in 1871, took Holy Orders, as did many Victorian schoolmasters.

While at Cheltenham, he was the Master of 'Christowe House' and in 1881 the census shows that he and Julia had a matron and seven servants to cope with forty one boarders aged between thirteen and eighteen.

Two years later, at the age of thirty seven, he became the Headmaster of Oundle School in Northamptonshire where he remained for about a year until ill-health affected him and forced his resignation from the school. Today Oundle is the third largest Public School in England.

After a period of two and a half years, he felt ready to return to teaching. He applied for the position of Headmaster at Berkhamsted School and was successful, starting there in 1888.

During the following twenty-two years he was largely responsible for the very considerable development of the school, both in terms of building, staffing, attainment and support. The number of pupils at the school increased from one hundred and sixty six to four hundred and sixty three. Whereas there had been dormitory accommodation for eighty boarders, this was increased to house two hundred. The classroom and assembly area was quadrupled and a chapel, a gymnasium and a swimming bath were added. The staffing of nine masters was increased to twenty-one and these were certainly better paid and ready to spend their days at Berkhamsted, more so than many of their predecessors had been.

One of the staff who came to the school at the end of 1888, during the first year of Dr Fry's term of office, was Charles Henry Greene, an appointment clearly brought about by the family relationship. He arrived at the school as a temporary replacement for a master who was ill. It was six months after leaving Oxford and three days after his twenty fourth birthday. He remained there for thirty eight years, the last sixteen as Headmaster. It was his original intention to become a solicitor.

He was recorded, aged twenty six, on the 1891 Census living in a lodging house in Berkhamsted High Street. Another assistant master also lodged there. Charles had no experience of working in any other school and learned everything from Dr Fry, both the skills of teaching and the art of planning and administration.

He had a successful career at the school, becoming a close friend and confidante of the headmaster. In 1894 he was made housemaster of St John's and, two years later, became second master.

In 1895 he had married a cousin, Marion Raymond Greene, the daughter of Carleton Greene, vicar of Great Barford in Bedfordshire, who was herself a first cousin of the author, Robert Louis Stevenson.

Charles and Marion lived in St John's House in Chesham Road

where their children were born. Their daughter, Alice Marion (Molly), was born there in 1897 and their eldest son, (William) Herbert followed in 1898. Their son, (Charles) Raymond Greene, was born in 1901, followed by (Henry) Graham Greene in 1904 and Hugh Carleton Greene in 1910. Finally Elisabeth (Katherine) was born in 1914.

During the Easter holidays, Marion Greene and her children, with their nurse, would travel by train to Littlehampton to enjoy the seaside. They had a third class reserved compartment in which they ate their 'hamper' lunch. Charles would travel alone, a few days later, second class! He seemed distantly aloof and separated from his children in their early years.

In the Summer holidays, the family went to Harston, situated between Royston in Hertfordshire and Cambridge on the A10. There, they would stay in 'Harston House', the home of Charles' brother, William Graham Greene. William remained in his London flat in Park Lane, when such visits took place!

Parts of 'Harston House', or 'Harston Hall' as it was formerly known, date back to Roman times, although its main building is seventeenth century. 'Harston House' was very large and had an old-fashioned garden with a fountain on the front lawn. There was a stream and a pond containing an island. The garden was very overgrown in places with many trees and, in all, made an excellent play area for young children.

In 1910, Thomas Fry decided that the time was right for leaving Berkhamsted to become the Dean of Lincoln. This he did and he remained there until he died in February, 1930. Many people remembered him as being an outstanding, even great, headmaster.

On the resignation of Dr Fry, Charles Greene was appointed as Headmaster. Dr Fry was delighted at his appointment, having done all in his power to ensure that this happened!

Charles and his family were recorded on the 1911 Census living in the "School House". They had eight servants and a matron to look after them and sixty two boarders. With them was Thomas H C Hopkins, aged thirty four, a former pupil who had been appointed as a master in 1902 by Dr Fry. Shortly after this he was destined to fight in the First World War when he became a major. He returned after the war and became the house master of 'Incent's House' in 1919.

Charles had followed in the footsteps of his mentor but he was undoubtedly 'his own man'. Dr Fry was an extremely conscientious and efficient teacher and administrator who had achieved undoubted success. Charles was an outstanding teacher who set his mind to providing the school with many of the things that were lacking when he took over as headmaster.

His first major triumph was the acquisition of new playing fields, badly needed by the school. This he achieved with the help of his brother, Edward, who proved to be a tower of strength to both Charles and the school.

Charles was able to reduce the size of classes, appoint an art master, revive the debating society, and arrange for lectures on political and cultural subjects. There were notable academic successes, as well as more on the fields of sport.

All was progressing well in the pre-war years and Charles Greene, in spite of many doubts over his appointment, proved himself to his critics.

While the early years of his time as headmaster of Berkhamsted School had been relatively smooth, the war years proved a difficult time for him and for the school in general.

By the Summer of 1916 no more than half of the twenty six men previously on the staff were still there. During the course of the war, thirty two men and women were appointed to the staff. Very few lasted more than a year and the inexperience and incompetence of many substitutes placed a huge strain on regular members of staff who remained at the school, not least the headmaster.

In July 1918 Greene announced that one thousand four hundred and forty five Old Berkhamstedians were serving, or had served, in the war. One hundred and eighty four had been killed and one hundred and seventeen wounded. One hundred and twenty one had been mentioned in despatches, seventy-eight had been awarded the MC, seventeen the DSO and one the VC. Less than a week before the

Armistice the figure of deaths approached two hundred and thirty and another VC was awarded.

Undoubtedly the loss of these men had a profound effect on the headmaster but his feelings were not communicated and he ensured that the school continued to progress steadily throughout the war years.

After the war there was a shortage of funding. Higher salaries were sought by staff, the number of pupils was increasing and more accommodation was required. It took several years for any real stability to be obtained on the staff, only one of his wartime appointments remaining on a permanent basis.

Funds were raised, money was borrowed and gifts were made which enabled the governing body to build additional classrooms and provide more playing fields.

Once again, Charles's brother, Edward Greene, was able to help. He presented his property known as the 'Old' or 'Upper Mill' to the School. This, together with the acquisition of other properties in Mill Street, through the generosity of the Old Boys Association, made way for a development north and north-west of the existing buildings. The Music School and Fives Courts were built on the site.

In 1925 Charles Greene had reached the age of sixty, the normal time for retirement, He had been persuaded by the governors to stay longer in order to solve some of the outstanding problems at the school and so he remained for a further two years.

Not surprisingly, his brother, Edward, had been co-opted as a governor of the school. In Charles's last term he advised the Governors that he had received a letter from his brother offering the school the freehold meadow adjoining the Preparatory School playground to remain as an open space for all time, suggesting that it should be known as 'Greene Fields' in memory of his brother's work for the school.

Undoubtedly, Charles had been an excellent headmaster, efficient in his administration and inspiring in his leadership. His teaching was of the highest standard and, no doubt, Dr Fry was delighted with the contribution that his successor had made to Berkhamsted School.

It is worth noting that Charles, a man of determination and a very successful administrator had not inherited these qualities from his father. He had, however, acquired the love of literature that his father had so enjoyed. Charles became a Fellow of the Royal Historical Society and retired to Crowborough in Sussex where he died in 1942.

Edward Greene

Charles's brother, Edward, born in 1866, sought to make a fortune abroad. In 1891 he arrived in Brazil to work in the coffee industry. He joined the firm of E. Johnston & Co.

Edward Johnston, a Londoner, arrived in Rio in 1821. He founded the company twenty one years later and in 1853 took his son into partnership. In 1842, half of the exports of cotton, sugar and coffee from Brazil were undertaken by British firms.

After Johnston's death in 1876, the firm was run by his sons and a branch of the business was opened in Santos, the port of Sao Paulo. It was here that Edward Greene joined the firm. His ability was soon recognised. His business acumen, the sharpness of his mind and the nerve shown in his work, led to his being offered a partnership four years later in 1895.

In 1906, he created a warehousing company to be used in Brazil and in the United Kingdom, giving the firm a tremendous advantage in trading. He became the eventual driving force in the company and, four years later, he formed the Brazilian Warrant Company to control warehousing and offer private loans to coffee makers. He returned to England to run the business.

While in Brazil, he had married Eva, a German girl, and they had two sons and two daughters, born there between 1902 and 1908. His youngest son was born in 1910 in Berkhamsted.

In 1910, when he arrived back in England, he decided to live near his brother, Charles, and rented a large property known as 'Elvyne Hall' in Chesham Road, Berkhamsted. 'Elvyne' was owned by Lt. Colonel Henry James Foster who lived in another large house close by. 'Elvyne' stood in one and a quarter acres of woodland and had a value assessed at £1,500 in 1912. Edward and his family were recorded at this address on the 1911 Census. Edward's wife was not there and Edward's unmarried sister, Alice, aged 53, was with him and his children, a cook, a nurse and a maid.

Shortly after this, Edward purchased a property known as 'The Hall', situated on the London Road, Berkhamsted and the property known as 'Elvyne Hall', in which he and his family had lived, was acquired by Berkhamsted School and used as the Preparatory School boarding house.

'The Hall' was a Georgian mansion, the largest in Berkhamsted, having seventeen bedrooms and dressing rooms. It was enclosed in high walls and built in extensive grounds. The rear view of the property was much more attractive than that seen from the London Road. This property was one of several purchased in Berkhamsted by Edward Greene after his arrival in the town.

Before the First World War began, Edward, giving support to his brother, offered the governors of the school a substantial amount of money towards providing for new playing fields that were urgently required. It was his generosity, followed by a huge effort on the part of the governors to raise the balance of money required, that allowed this development to take place.

After the War, in 1922, he gave another of his properties, the 'Old Mill', to the School, as stated above.

The Brazilian Warrant Company, having an international governing body, amalgamated with other companies and formed a multi-national organisation. The Brazilian Warrant Company held a majority of the shares with a recorded capital of over £1,500,000. Edward Greene had become a very rich man.

In 1924 E Johnston & Co was described as the largest British exporting firm in the country. Edward was fifty eight at this time and he lived to the age of seventy two.

In 1928, after the retirement of Charles Greene, the Governors acquired 'The Hall' and some of the surrounding land, no longer occupied by Edward Greene but still owned by him, as a base for the Preparatory School. 'Elvyne Hall' then became the school's sanatorium and later a boarding house that had to close eventually because of decreasing numbers of pupils.

Unfortunately, in the 1930s, 'The Hall' was found to be infested with dry rot and was later pulled down, the land being sold on the open market and the school suffered a substantial loss that could have been avoided if a proper survey had been carried out earlier.

The whole estate was vast and much of the land was sold to allow the development of council estates. Several of the roads in the area reflect the name of Hall.

Edward Greene, had shown great generosity towards the School, in support of his brother, but he never lost his business acumen and those characteristics that had served him well in his days in Brazil and afterwards. Certainly he had followed in the footsteps of his grandfather, Benjamin, and showed many of his qualities.

The Greene Family in Berkhamsted
The Children of Charles Henry and Marion Greene

William Herbert Greene
Charles and Marion's eldest son, (William) Herbert Greene, born in 1898, did not achieve the success or fame of his younger brothers. He inherited the adventurous nature of members of the Greene family, particularly as a child, but his later life was filled with a number of failures, as was his grandfather's. He edited the 'School House' Gazette at Berkhamsted and towards the end of the First World War he became a Lance Corporal in the Honourable Artillery Company but he never reached France. In the 1930s he served, without any great success, as a spy for the Imperial Japanese Navy. Little else has been recorded of his life.

Herbert's younger brothers were baptised as (Charles) Raymond, (Henry) Graham and Hugh Carleton Greene. They all became exceptionally well-known in England and, indeed, throughout the world. It is not within the context of this work to discuss their achievements at length but only to look at some of the connections made by them, both within and outside of their family and, particularly, in Hertfordshire.

Charles Raymond Greene

Raymond, was born in Berkhamsted in 1901. He was born in St John's in Chesham Road where his father was the Housemaster. When his father was made headmaster in 1910, the family moved to the 'School House' which was a part of the original school building in Castle Street behind the thirteenth century Norman Church.

At the age of eleven, he transferred from his family, living in 'School House', back to 'St John's' where he became Head of House and a School Prefect. He had an excellent school record and went up to Pembroke College, Oxford, where he studied Medicine, before moving to Westminster Hospital where he qualified in 1927. He became an MA, an MD and a FRCP. He was an expert in the treatment of thyroid and other diseases of the endocrine system, as well as migraine and frostbite.

While still at school, he climbed in the Lake District and, when at Oxford, he went to the Alps and later to the Himalayas. He was a very competent mountaineer and was the Senior Doctor of the fourth British Expedition to Mount Everest in 1933.

He was both a writer and a broadcaster. When Everest was finally climbed in 1953, Raymond Greene made the announcement on the BBC.

He was the first of the Greene family to study medicine and to achieve such a distinguished career. His love of mountaineering came through his connections at school in Berkhamsted with a fellow pupil. The desire to explore and conquer unknown territory was seen in many members of his family, certainly back to the time of his great grandfather, Benjamin.

There is no doubt that his writing and broadcasting skills in later years were, to a large extent, gained from the work of his younger brothers. He was married and had a son and daughter. He died in

December 1982, aged eighty one.

Henry Graham Greene

Graham, was born in 1904. Again, his early years were spent in 'St John's House' before his father was made Headmaster.

In his book, 'A Sort of Life' he writes of happy days playing in the gardens of 'St John's' and at 'The Hall', the home of his uncle, Edward Greene, known as 'Eppy', who had six children, his cousins.

The time spent with his mother appears to have been very limited. After tea, the children would go down from their nursery or playroom, just for an hour, to play with their mother. Usually, she would read them a story. At other times they were in the care of a nanny or a nursery-maid. Their father was even more remote, spending much of his time in his study working on the organisation of the school.

During one of the family holidays at Harston, Graham found that he could read. He hid his new found talent from his family and read in secret. However, his ability did not go unnoticed by his mother. His love of reading intensified as he grew older and, obviously, played a significant part in his future writing.

At the age of thirteen, after three years in the Junior School, Graham returned to 'St John's House' as a boarder. The circumstances of his happier early years changed to a time of extreme unhappiness. He felt threatened because his father was the Headmaster and because his brother was Head of the House. He believed that others thought of him as 'spying' on behalf of his family. He was unable to make friends for fear of letting his father or his brother down. He was not subjected to any physical abuse but his sensitivity and vivid imagination led to periods of deep depression and hatred of some boys.

It should be noted that, as well as his older brother, his cousins were also pupils in the school and suffered no similar difficulties.

The somewhat Spartan existence of the boarding house was intolerable for him. At this time, both bullying and primitive conditions were seen as a toughening-up process in Public Schools with an aim of turning boys into men, a practice which seems to have continued through the years.

Graham had no liking for physical activities such as cricket and rugby football and felt even more isolated and unpopular as a result. He invented excuses to avoid such activities, often truanting to find a quiet place to read his books.

For eighteen terms he endured monotony, humiliation and mental pain. No longer could he stand the interminable repetition and boredom of his education and he made the decision to 'run away'.

What he actually did was to leave a note stating that he would not return until his parents agreed that he would not be forced to return to 'St John's'. Following this he went to hide on Berkhamsted Common. Some two hours later he came face to face with his elder sister, Molly, who was searching for him. She took him home without any fuss. Nevertheless, Graham felt refreshed and happy to have made his protest.

His parents, concerned by his action, sent for Raymond, then studying medicine in Oxford, to help them in choosing a course of action. They decided that Graham should have psycho-analysis.

He spent the next six months at the house of his analyst, Kenneth Richmond, in London where he was served breakfast in bed in a warm and very comfortable environment! He describes his stay there as perhaps the happiest time of his life as it was a complete contrast to Berkhamsted. He was given the independence to go into the West End and visit cinemas and theatres. He developed his love of literature and history, as he was introduced to a circle of his analyst's literary friends and he was encouraged to write, to express his thoughts, feelings and ambitions.

When Graham returned to Berkhamsted, he was no longer required to go to 'St John's'. He was socially more confident and made friends easily. His fears of his former days had gone as he worked in the sixth form and prepared for entry to Oxford University.

He entered Balliol College in 1922 to study modern history. He developed an interest in politics and joined the Communist Party out of interest or curiosity rather than conviction. It was not long before he realised that his feelings of boredom and acute depression were still with him. He writes that in order to find some excitement in his life, he indulged in Russian roulette, in isolation, using a pistol found in his brother's cupboard. He survived several attempts but slowly the exhilaration wore off and the adrenalin no longer flowed. At a later stage in his life he realised that he had inherited many of his paternal grandfather's emotions and characteristics.

While at Balliol he wrote poems, stories, reviews and articles for the Oxford Outlook, a student magazine.

After graduating from Oxford in 1925, and some fruitless work experience, Graham was employed as an editorial trainee by the Nottingham Journal. While there he met his future wife, Vivien Dayrell-Browning. She persuaded him to take instruction in her Catholic faith and he was received into the Church in 1926.

He took a post as a sub-editor at The Times and married Vivien in 1927. They had a daughter and a son. All the time, he was writing and submitting his work for publication. The acceptance of 'The Man Within' in 1929 led to his leaving The Times and becoming a full-time writer, not successfully in the early stages.

He wrote, 'A real person stands in the way of imagination. Perhaps a trick of speech, a physical trait may be used, but I can write no more than a few pages before realizing that I simply don't know enough about the character to use him, even if he is an old friend – with the imaginary character I am sure.' (Ways of Escape pp 255 -8)

In Berkhamsted he imagined the faces of the townsfolk, people he was unable to know or control, to show the evil that was in them.

He used his childhood memories of holidays in Harston to create an imaginary underground island dwelling in a short story, 'Under the Garden', in his work, 'A Sense of Reality'.

Again, in the preface to 'The Human Factor', published in 1978, he quotes Hans Christian Andersen, – 'out of reality are our tales of imagination fashioned'. 'The Human Factor', is a novel about a double agent, Maurice Castle, who lives in Kings Road, Berkhamsted, two roads from where Greene was born. Castle commutes to London where he works for the 'Secret Service'.

Greene's uncle had helped to establish a naval intelligence department. His brother, Herbert, had acted as a spy in the 1930s, and his younger sister, Elisabeth, had joined MI6 and had recruited Graham into the service during World War II. He had an intimate knowledge of the affairs of the secret service and was also a close friend of Kim Philby, the double agent, but denied that Maurice Castle was based on him.

The novel illustrates Greene's use of reality in imaginative terms as he describes Castle taking his young son through the town centre of Berkhamsted, past the school, to the Castle and to Berkhamsted Common; all familiar scenes of his own childhood.

In 'The Captain and the Enemy', published in 1988, the unhappy experiences of Victor Baxter in his days at school reflect Greene's days in Berkhamsted as he examines the nature of truth and true love, deception and reality between the Captain and Lisa.

In his writing he continues to explore the conflicting themes of Evil and Good, the existence of God and the Devil, Love and Hate, Communism and Catholicism, spying, treachery and betrayal, as all of the experiences of his life, both at home and throughout the world are given to the imaginary characters of his creation.

Like the Greene family before him, he inherited a significant desire to travel throughout the world. His journeys satisfied his longing for adventure, change and the defeat of boredom, at the same time as providing him with material for his writing. He travelled extensively from Sweden to Mexico, to Liberia, Vietnam and Kenya, Poland and Cuba.

He wrote more than twenty novels, many of which have been filmed, as well as collections of short stories, travel books, plays, three autobiographies, two biographies, four children's books and numerous essays. He became one the best-loved and most prolific and widely read of the novelists writing in the 20th Century and his work may be purchased from leading bookshops today, not just in WH Smith's or Waterstone's in Berkhamsted!

He had separated from his wife in 1948 and had many extra-marital affairs in the years that followed. He lived in London, Antibes and Capri. In 1959 he met Yvonne Cloetta while in Doula in Cameroon. There began a relationship which lasted for over thirty years. He spent his final days in Providence Hospital in Vevey, Switzerland, where he died in April 1991.

Hugh Carleton Greene

Hugh Carleton Greene was born in 1910. Carleton was the maiden name of his maternal great, great grandmother, Elizabeth Smith.

Like his brothers, he was educated at Berkhamsted before going to university. He went up to Merton College, Oxford where he obtained an MA.

On leaving Oxford in 1933 he became a news correspondent for The New Statesman and the Daily Herald before becoming the chief correspondent of the Daily Telegraph in Germany in 1934 reporting on the development of Nazi Germany.

In October 1934 he married Helga Mary Guinness of the famous brewing family.

He was expelled from Berlin in 1939 but continued to report on the beginning of World War II from Warsaw. In 1940 he joined the BBC as Head of the German Service. He made some significant improvements in broadcasting and he became 'a familiar face' in presenting news and featuring in discussion programmes.

He and Mary were divorced in 1948, having had two sons, Graham and James. He received an OBE in 1950 before he married Elaine Shaplen in 1951. They had two sons.

His ability in a variety of posts did not go unnoticed and he was made Director of Administration before becoming Director of News and Current Affairs. In 1960 he was appointed as Director General of the BBC.

He kept pace with the changes of the 1960s and introduced controversial programmes on Television dealing with the social issues of the time. These programmes were critical of society, often through comedy. Programmes that questioned values, that dealt with political and current affairs were introduced. This completely transformed the image of the BBC which had always steered clear of anything unconventional or controversial.

Of course, his changes brought him many enemies, notably Mary Whitehouse, and there was, indeed, considerable opposition towards his policy of change. He showed great determination in dealing with this while he continued to modernise broadcasting in this country.

He was made a Knight Commander of St Michael and St George in 1964.

In 1967, under his policy for change, Radio 1 broadcast pop music for the first time. Hugh brought forward new ideas and new methods as well as introducing new talent.

During his time as Director General, BBC 2, Colour Television, BBC Local Radio and Radios 1 – 4 were introduced.

In 1968 he announced that he would retire from the corporation, following the appointment of a new Chairman of Governors who was destined to ensure that a more conservative and less provocative approach was adopted in broadcasting.

His determination to succeed, to make changes and to improve the service of broadcasting, together with his sharpness of mind in business administration were the qualities that had been seen in both his father and his great grandfather.

Apparently, apart from his broadcasting and writing, he also was known for his appreciation of beer, although he had had nothing to do with the production of this.

It was not surprising then that, in 1964, Sir Hugh Carleton Greene became a Director of the Greene King Brewery in Bury. In 1971 he took over as Chairman and remained in that position until 1978 when his son succeeded him.

When he died in 1987 he was described as the man who made the modern BBC.

The Priestley Family in London and Northaw

As stated, Elizabeth Hall married Hugh Priestley on 26th January 1911. The Priestley Family can be traced back to the middle of the 18th Century living in the small town of Birstall, situated between Leeds and Dewsbury in West Yorkshire. It was here that Hugh's five times great grandfather, Joseph, was married to Mary Longbottom in 1766. Mary's family can be traced in the area of the village of Liversedge back to 1634.

Hugh's grandfather, William Overend Priestley, was born in 1829 in Birstall. He became a physician with an MD from Edinburgh and worked as an obstetrician in Edinburgh and London.

His son Robert Chambers Priestley, born in 1857 in Westminster, was a BA Cantab and, as a student, lived with his father at 17 Hertford Street, a turning off Piccadilly in London. They were recorded at this address on the 1881 Census with a butler, a footman, a cook and three domestic servants.

Following his father, Robert also became a physican. He married and his son, Hugh William, was born on 19th September, 1887 in Marylebone, London.

In 1891 Hugh was living with his brother, Edward, aged one, and their grandmother, Eliza Priestley, who was born in Edinburgh. Their address was Warrior Square, Hastings.

At the age of thirteen, Hugh was at a private boarding school in Remesham Place, Wokingham, Berkshire. The Headmaster was a clergyman and he, together with his wife and four daughters, lived in the school with a governess and two tutors. There were twenty nine pupils between the ages of nine and thirteen residing there as well as a domestic staff of thirteen.

Hugh was living at 81 Linden Gardens, Bayswater and was a stockbroker at the time he married Elizabeth (Elsie) Grainger Hall, the second daughter of Frederic and Elizabeth Hall of 'Northaw Place'. The ceremony, conducted by Elizabeth's uncle, the Reverend George T. Hall, took place in Northaw Church on 26th January 1911.

After the wedding, Hugh and Elsie lived in 'Northaw Place' with the Hall family. They were recorded there on the 1911 Census.

Hugh served in the Army in the First World War. He joined the London Regiment and was made a lieutenant in September 1914. He was promoted to the rank of captain when the regiment was shipped to France in January 1917 and in June 1918 he became a major as part of the British Expeditionary Force. He was seriously wounded in August 1918 and returned to England in September of that year. He had severe injuries to his chest, his right arm, his left leg and his forehead. He was awarded the Military Cross. He persuaded his superior officers to allow him to rejoin his regiment after a long period of convalescence and he became a staff captain of the 8th Battalion of the London Regiment from April to July in 1921.

After the First World War, Hugh returned to his life as a stockbroker in London.

He died at his London home, 51 Montague Square, London W1. on 8th January 1932. He was forty four and had contracted 'flu which turned to pneumonia from which he never recovered. He was buried in Northaw churchyard, next to the grave of Frederic Hall, his father-in-law.

After Hugh's death, Elsie lived in a flat on the top floor of a house in Kensington near Cottesmore Gardens.

The Children of Hugh Priestley and Elizabeth Grainger Hall

Hugh and Elsie had three sons, the grandchildren of Frederic and Elizabeth Hall of 'Northaw Place'.

Robert

Robert Hugh, their eldest son, was born on 23rd December 1911. He was educated at Winchester College before going up to Trinity College Cambridge to study Law from 1930 to 1932 after which he joined the firm of Mullens & Co, London Stockbrokers. In April 1935 he married Mary Hermia, the daughter of Sir George Menteth

Boughey CBE, the 9th Baronet. In 1936 he was a member of the London Stock Exchange.

He joined the Territorial Army and became a 2nd Lieutenant in the Royal Corps of Signals in 1939. He served in the MEF from 1940 until 1943 and was made a Captain in 1941. In 1943 he was at the staff college in Haifa. He served in Sicily and Italy between 1943 and 1944 as a Major. From 1944 to 1945 he was in NW Europe and was awarded an MBE. He was twice mentioned in despatches and was awarded the Bronze Star medal of the USA. After the War, he became a partner in Mullens & Co and lived in Basingstoke.

James

James Frederick (Jimmie), their second son, was born 22nd February, 1915. Like his brother, he was a Wykehamist. He also studied at Western Reserve Academy, Hudson in the USA in 1933.

In 1934 he joined Wedd, Jefferson & Co., stock jobbers.

He was a 2nd Lieutenant in the Territorial Army, Hertfordshire Regiment, in 1939 when he married Honor Purefoy, the daughter of Robert Pollock of London. He transferred to the Coldstream Guards in 1940 and received the Commander in Chief's Certificate for Good Service in 1943. From D Day until 1946 he served in North West Europe as a major and was awarded the Military Cross. After the War, he rejoined Wedd Jefferson and became a partner in 1946. In 1968 he was a director of his firm which became Wedd Durlacher Mordaunt. He lived in Andover and Winchester.

He and Honor had a son, Hugh Michael, born in 1942 who, again, went to Winchester before going to Worcester College, Oxford where he obtained an MA in Modern Langauges in 1964.

Another son, Richard James, born in 1947, was also educated at Winchester. He studied at Grenoble University in France before joining his brother's stock-jobbing firms. He worked and lived in London.

Tony

The third son of Hugh and Elizabeth, Anthony Victor (Tony), was born on 17th November 1918. Another Wykehamist, he was in the

RMC in 1936 and a 2nd Lieutenant in the Coldstream Guards in 1938. He served in the BEF from 1939 to 1940 when he was wounded. He was in the UK from 1940 to 1944. In 1942 he married Lois Rose Mary, daughter of Brigadier General WGH Thompson CGM DSO.

He returned to NW Europe in 1944 when he was wounded again. He became a Staff Captain. Later he joined the firm of Deuchar, brewers of Newcastle. He died at the age of 46.

The Devitt Family –
Northaw and Pangbourne in Berkshire

Dorothy Hall, the daughter of Frederic and Elizabeth Hall of Shirburn, married Philip Henry Devitt on 22nd February 1919.

Philip's grandfather, Thomas Henry Devitt, was born on 25th March 1800, the son of Andrew and Elizabeth Devitt of Newry, Co. Down in Ireland. He was born in Yarmouth on the Isle of Wight. He was educated privately in Southampton before going to London where he gained valuable experience working with merchants and shipowners.

In 1836 Thomas Devitt and Joseph Moore, a fellow shipping clerk, decided to set up a shipbroking firm of their own. In the beginning this firm, Devitt & Moore, was quite a small concern but it was developed through much hard work and enthusiasm.

Thomas married Margaret Lane on 6th February 1838 in Hackney, London. Margaret was the second daughter of Brazillai Lane of Lansdown Park, Hackney.

The 1841 census recorded the couple with their children, Thomas Lane Devitt, aged two, who was to be Philip's father, and Frank of nine months. Thomas was recorded as a ship insurance broker and was living in Sydney Place, Bethnal Green.

Ten years later, the family had moved to Lansdowne House, Margaret's former home, in Dalston, Hackney. Thomas was fifty one and Margaret was thirty six. Their sons, Thomas and Frank, were with them as well as three more sons, Henry, Joseph and Andrew, and three daughters, Emma, Bessie and Fanny. They employed four servants.

Thomas Henry Devitt died in 1860 and Joseph Moore offered his son, Thomas Lane Devitt, then aged twenty, a partnership in the firm of Devitt & Moore.

Thomas and Margaret's eldest son, Thomas Lane Devitt, was educated at Madras House Grammar School in Hackney and Sherborne College in Dorset. He married Fanny Theodora, the daughter of the late Ebenezer Pye Smith F. R.C.S on 25th February 1863.

In that year Devitt & Moore expanded into actually owning sailing ships. However the future was seen to be in steamships and in 1870 the company bought one. This venture ended in disaster when the ship ran aground and was a total loss. It was a devastating experience for those working in the company, although no lives were lost, and it certainly changed their thinking for the future. Thomas never lost his love of sailing ships although he realised that steam would eventually prevail.

Throughout his life and his love for the sea and ships, he sought to improve the training of British merchant seamen. Rather than having apprentices, nearly always used as cheap labour on ships at sea, his aim was to give proper instruction on board training ships used specifically for this purpose. Training schemes were formulated and thousands of men were trained to a high standard on two ships designated solely for this purpose.

In 1871 Thomas Lane Devitt's mother, Margaret, was living at 'The Place' in Clapton High Road. She was fifty six and her daughters, Emma, Bessie, Fanny and Margaret and sons, Andrew, a clerk, and Charles, were with her. A cook and two domestic servants were in the household.

Thomas and Fanny were recorded in 1871 living in 'Spring Hill House', Stamford Hill, Hackney. Their first child, a daughter, Mary Theodora, died as an infant in 1864 but by the time of this census they had several young children. Helen Margaret was five, Emily four, Arthur three, Howson Foulger was one, and Lilian Dorothea was five months. Thomas, described as a shipowner and broker, employed a cook, two nurses, two housemaids and a gardener.

In 1878, in spite of his earlier experience, Thomas became a steamship owner and joined with two other companies to found the Orient Line, a company which dominated the sea route to Australia for more than half a century.

By 1881 Thomas and Fanny had three more of their children living with them. Herbert Pye Smith, aged seven, Philip Henry, five, and Katherine Rutherford, who was one. They were employing a governess, a cook, two nurses and two maids.

After Preparatory School, Thomas sent his sons to be educated at Sherborne School in Dorset. This was the school that he had attended. They matriculated from there and followed one another to Trinity Hall, Cambridge where they graduated before becoming highly successful in a number of different professions.

Thomas had taken over the running of his company as Joseph Moore and his son ceased to be so actively involved. Two new full-rigged ships, to be managed by Devitt & Moore, were bought from the Orient Line for training purposes and, between 1890 and 1918, more than six hundred cadets were given an education and training in seamanship. The outbreak of the War in 1914 severely curtailed what could be achieved and this led to a new development taking place.

Thomas believed implicitly in the need of a good education for those young men about to make a career at sea. He saw that a change in the system was necessary in that a two-year training at a nautical school, before going to sea on a training ship, would ensure that only those with the right qualities would be selected.

He had devoted his life entirely to his world of shipping as the following paragraphs show. He was twice Master of The Skinners Company from 1885 to 1886 and from 1896 to 1897. From 1896 until 1900 he was an Elected Member of Lloyds and also a Trustee. At this time his business was at 2 White Lion Court, Cornhill, London.

The 1901 Census recorded Fanny, living at 'Sandlea House' in Datchet, Buckinghamshire. With her was Helen, unmarried, as well as Howson, single, an Insurance Broker at Lloyds, and Philip, an Articled Solicitors Clerk. Fanny had a cook and maids. Thomas was not with them when the census was taken.

In 1911, at the age of seventy two, Thomas was living with Fanny at 16 Cumberland Terrace, St Pancras. Helen and Philip, both unmarried, were with them as were a footman, a cook, a 'sick nurse' and three maids.

Thomas was president of The Institute of Shipbrokers and Senior Partner in the firm of Devitt and Moore, Master of the Shipwrights Company in 1917 and Chairman of Lloyds Register of Shipping from 1909 to 1920 and was President of the Institute of Marine Engineers from 1913 to 1914.

In recognition of his service, Thomas was created a Baronet in July, 1916. In that year, at the age of seventy six, he set out to find a suitable place for a nautical school to be started. He was looking for an establishment close to an estuary where a training ship could be moored close by.

His search resulted in his finding Pangbourne, on the Thames, near Reading. This was the Bere Hill estate which had been owned by various persons and used for a variety of purposes. In 1902, it was sold to Alexander Devine who converted the existing house and added a variety of buildings as well as providing many sports facilities for the pupils of Clayesmore School which he started there. It became necessary for him to move the school and this gave the opportunity for Thomas to purchase the site for £10,000. In addition to this, he had to pay an additional £2000 for the purchase of 'Thames Cottage', with a river frontage, in order to gain access to the River Thames. Within a year, the new Pangbourne Nautical College was opened for the training of cadets. Henry's son, Philip, played a large part in acquiring this building and in the foundation of the college.

After gaining his BA degree in 1889, Thomas' eldest son, Arthur, became a Shipbroker working with his father in Fenchurch Street, London. He married Florence Emmeline Gordon in 1897. She was living at 'Great Cozens', Ware, in Hertfordshire, although she was born in New South Wales. They had a daughter, Mary, born in 1899 in Englefield Green, Surrey and a son, Thomas Gordon, born in 1902. At this time, the family was living in 'Shelley's Cottage', Bishopsgate, Egham in Surrey. Arthur's brother, Herbert Pye-Smith Devitt, was living with them.

Thomas's wife, Fanny, died on 5th February, 1917, in Chelsea, and her son, Arthur, died in 1921.

Arthur's son, Thomas Gordon, educated like his father at Sherborne School, became a school prefect and played in the school cricket team for three years, He also played Rugby in the First Fifteen for three years and was made captain in his final year. He went to Corpus Christi College Cambridge where he played Rugby for the university for three years. After this he played for Blackheath RFC and for the Seaforth Highlanders when he was a lieutenant in the 1st Battalion. He was selected to play 'on the wing' for England. He made his debut against Ireland at Lansdowne Road in February 1926. He also played against France and Wales in 1928 when the team won 'The Championship'. He was capped four times, winning in three of the matches and losing in one. He didn't score a try!

While at Cambridge he had inherited the Baronetcy in 1923, following the death of his grandfather at the age of eighty four on 8th December of that year. He became Thomas Gordon Devitt 2nd Baronet of Chelsea. He married Joan Freemantle of Hayes Barton, Pyrford in Surrey in 1930.

Arthur's brother, Howson Foulger Devitt, married Winifred Woollcombe in 1908 in London. They had two sons and twin daughters and the family lived in Sevenoaks in Kent. Their Insurance Company was Howson F. Devitt & Sons. Their son, Howson Charles, born in 1909, served as a Wing Commander in the War. He was awarded an OBE and later lived at Ingatestone in Essex. He was Philip's godson. Another son, Peter, born in 1911, went to Sherborne School from 1924 until 1929. He became an insurance broker working with his father in London. He was a Wing Commander in the RAF and was mentioned in despatches. He lived in Limpsfield in Surrey.

Herbert, born in 1873, graduated from Trinity Hall College in 1898 and was made a Member of The Royal College of Surgeons and a Licentiate of the Royal College of Physicians in 1901. He worked in St George's Hospital in London and St Bartholomew's in Rochester. After retiring he lived in Gerrard's Cross, Buckinghamshire. His son, Philip Eyre Devitt, born in 1907, was sent to Sherborne School before going up to Caius College, Cambridge. He became a schoolmaster and played Rugby for Sussex. He became Headmaster of Falconbury School, Little Common, Bexhill in Sussex. Another son, Herbert, born in 1910 went to Trinity Hall College, Cambridge, as did their son, John Desmond Devitt. He worked in the Middlesex Hospital and was a Lieutenant in the RAMC. He was wounded and received the Silver Star of the USA. He lived in The Mount, Whitchurch in Hampshire.

In 1876 when Philip Henry, the youngest son of Thomas Lane Devitt, was born he had a squint in one eye. When he was three years old, an operation resulted in Philip not seeing from that eye again.

He was sent away to boarding school where he was educated in the first instance at Wymondley School in Hertfordshire where his future father-in-law was the headmaster.

In April 1890, he transferred to the Loretto School in Musselborough, near Edinburgh. He left two and a half years later. Loretto was a highly regarded educational establishment with an outstanding record then and remains so today.

From the Loretto School, he gained his place at Trinity Hall in Cambridge where he obtained an MA. He became an excellent oarsman, rowing for his college eight, and also for the Thames Rowing Club, taking part in the Grand Challenge Cup and the Stewards Cup at Henley.

In 1901 Philip was a solicitor's clerk with the firm, Nicol Son & Jones. He persevered with this work but was never really happy. Later he transferred to a firm of shipping lawyers in Cornhill, London. Finally he persuaded his father to let him join Devitt and Moore in 1906. He became a co-founder, with his father, of the new Pangbourne

Nautical College.

In 1911 he was unmarried and living with his mother, his father and his sister, Helen, who was also unmarried. They were recorded at 16 Cumberland Terrace, St Pancras on the census of that year when they employed a domestic staff of six.

Because of his loss of the sight of one eye, he was only able to serve as a Special Constable during the War. When he married Dorothy Hall, his address was given as 'The Priory', Leatherhead in Surrey. By this time he had become very involved in the life and management of Pangbourne.

Philip Devitt and Dorothy Hall

Their marriage took place in All Saints Church, Shirburn on 22nd February, 1919. The ceremony was conducted by the Vicar of Winchcombe, Reverend William F. Eliot, who was assisted by Reverend George Thomas Hall, Dorothy's uncle.

Many of the guests travelled to Oxfordshire by a special train from London. Lunch was served on the train. Lord Macclesfield lent Shirburn Castle to the Halls for a reception and life at the Vicarage was as usual. Dorothy milked the cows in the morning, as she had done throughout the war years! She had made the wedding cake and had to assemble the tiers of this in the castle at the same time as dealing with the large number of presents that had arrived.

She knew that to provide champagne for the large number of guests would be a cost that her father would find difficult to meet and so she ordered it herself, using the savings from her war-time pay, and the bottles were delivered to the castle, unknown to her father who thought they were a gift from the Macclesfield family.

An outbreak of rabies in the Scilly Isles prevented a planned honeymoon there and so Philip and Dorothy travelled to the Grand Hotel, Lyndhurst, in the New Forest. As neither bride nor groom drove a car, a chauffeur was hired to take them there where they spent their time going for long walks in the forest, getting wet and muddy!

The days of 'jetting off to the sun' had yet to come.

After their marriage, Philip and Dorothy lived in several different places, attempting to find a suitable property near to Pangbourne. At one time they lived in Twyford, on the outskirts of Reading, which was on the main railway line to London and a convenient journey to the offices of Devitt & Moore in Leadenhall Street. On another occasion they lived in Beaconsfield but in December 1919 they were living at 45, Montague Square in London when their eldest daughter, Theodora Joan, was born. She was baptised in Shirburn Church by Dorothy's father on 17th January 1920. Philip was shown in the register as a Shipowner and Broker.

Theodora was born physically disabled and received tremendous support from her family throughout her life. Little was known about her condition at this time and the amount of love and affection she received was quite remarkable, not in the least from both sets of her grandparents. Frequent visits had to be made to hospitals to see specialists and to receive whatever help was available. Fortunately her parents were able to employ a governess to care for her.

Philip and Dorothy continued to seek a suitable house and another daughter, Elizabeth Anne, was born and baptised in the church at Shirburn in 1921 when her parents were living at Beach Cottage in Aldeburgh.

Finally Philip found the home that they sought. It was called 'Foxholes' and was in Pirton Road just outside of Hitchin.

'Foxholes' was, and still is, a large Victorian house built in or about 1877 for William Tindall Lucas, a member of the well-known Quaker family who had been living in the Hitchin area for more than two hundred years before that time.

'Foxholes' was sold to Philip H. Devitt in, or about, 1921. It was a large red-bricked house, approached by a circular driveway that enclosed a lawn with a sun dial in the centre. This was replaced by a fountain at a later time. The house was built with three storeys. There was an oak-panelled entrance hall, off which was a small morning room, as well as a drawing room, a dining room and a billiard room, all facing south and overlooking the beautiful terraced garden with sloping lawns and grass banks. The porch and the flower room faced north. A wide oak staircase led up to the family bedrooms, guest rooms and the nurseries, as well as the servants' rooms.

There was a day nursery, in which the children played and ate their meals and a night nursery where they slept. The Devitts employed a nanny to care for the two girls. Another daughter, Jennifer Margaret, was born on 9th March 1923. She was baptised in St Mary's Church, Hitchin by her grandfather, Frederic Hall, on 20th May of that year. As the size of the family grew, the morning room downstairs was converted into a schoolroom and a governess was employed to teach the three girls. Then both upstairs nurseries were used for sleeping.

In the summertime, if the weather was fine, the children would have tea in the garden where there were tennis courts and an uncultivated area of trees and bushes to be explored. Next to a walled garden and a stable block was a part of 'Foxholes' known as the 'home farm' where pigs, cows and chickens were kept. Dorothy had already experienced milking cows while at Shirburn and she and the children, as they grew older, enjoyed taking an active part in caring for the animals there.

On occasions, either Dorothy, or the children's nanny and a nursemaid dressed in their uniforms of grey and white, would walk with the girls and prams into the market town of Hitchin, a distance of about a mile. In the years following there were fond memories of these visits when the girls recalled the toy shop, the chemist's and Barclays Bank, as well as St Mary's Church, where Philip and Dorothy were very active members of the congregation, and the Town Hall.

It is unlikely that they would have known that this town hall, where they often enjoyed bazaars and sales of work, had been built by the family who built 'Foxholes', nor would they have known that the man who had lived in 'Foxholes' before them was, at one time, a director of the Barclays Bank that stood before them in the Market Square.

The family remained at 'Foxholes' until it was decided that they should return to Northaw. The Devitt Family lived there until moving to Northaw in 1928.

In the early Thirties, 'Foxholes' was purchased by Hubert John Moss. Hubert was the son of William and Georgina Moss and was born in Hitchin in 1873. (see Moss Family)

Although Hubert and his wife maintained the house and grounds, they never actually lived in the house.

While remaining the property of Mr Moss, 'Foxholes' was requisitioned for use by The Maternity Section of the Mile End Road Hospital in London during the Second World War.

It was used as a 'rest home' for elderly men after the war and later, after it had remained empty for five years, it was acquired in 1960 by Assumptionists. Money was spent on adapting the house for its use in the training of young men for the priesthood. Assumptionist priests from all over Europe visited 'Foxholes'.

The house had over thirty rooms and could accommodate up to forty boys in two dormitories. There were two libraries, a recreation room and a dining room, as well as an excellent kitchen.

On one Sunday in the Summer of 1964, a service was broadcast from the chapel by the BBC Home Service. Annual fetes were held in the grounds and attracted many people from Hitchin and the neighbourhood, both Catholic and Non-Catholic.

In 1968 the training ended and the site was closed. However the Order maintained control for the time being.

Some time later, on September 13th, 1984, the property was advertised for sale in the Country Life Magazine. It was described as a spacious Victorian Mansion. It stated that the house was used as a Residential Training College.

In August 1996 the Oxford Archaeological Unit carried out a Field Evaluation on behalf of Ambleside Health Care Group, in respect of a Planning Application.

The unit found small pieces of pottery, animal bones, fragments of clay pipes, a knife handle, six nails, one button and fragments of iron and building materials. These were donated to the Hitchin Museum.

Since that time, 'Foxholes' has been used as a Nursing Home, with one change of ownership.

The Family of William Lucas – Hitchin

Long before 'Foxholes' was built for William Tindall Lucas, the family had established itself in Hitchin.

It has been traced back to the middle of the 16th Century. Family occupations are not stated until the beginning of the 18th Century but it is highly likely that they were millers and farmers in the Hitchin area.

Hitchin has always had many taverns and hostelries and ample breweries to sustain them because it is so close to an extensive barley growing area.

The most notable brewery was started by the Lucas family in 1709 in Angel Street (now Sun Street). The brewery functioned until it fell into disrepair in the 1920s and was taken over by J W Green Ltd of Luton who remained there for just three years. Finally the building was pulled down in 1963.

From this family of brewers came the well-established Quaker family of the 19th century. The family was undoubtedly very prosperous, building sumptuous houses in which to live, but also intent on being philanthropic and making a very considerable contribution to the enhancement of the lives of the poorer people of Hitchin.

The examples of their good work are too numerous to record in this context but reports of their achievement can be found in nearly all books recording the history of the town.

From the brothers Joseph and William Lucas, who ran the brewery initially, came the cousins Jeffrey, Edward and Francis, who all became greatly involved in the development of the bank in the years to come.

Many of the family had diverse talents. As an example, the lives of the sons of William Lucas are summarised below.

William Lucas, born in 1768, married Ann Bowlby of Cirencester on 15th November 1798. They had several children:

William

William was born on 4th June 1804 in Tilehouse Street, Hitchin.

The Grove, Highgate, London

Harston House, Cambridge

Berkhamsted School Gateway

Pangbourne College, Reading

Foxholes in Hitchin

Moss's Corner in Hitchin then

Moss's Corner in Hitchin now

Moss's in Ripon in Yorkshire

Moss's in Fenny Stratford, Buckinghamshire

SHARPLES BASSETT
& Co
BANKERS
ESTABLISHED HERE 1820
LATER
SHARPLES. TUKE. LUCAS
& SEEBOHM

AMALGAMATED WITH
BARCLAYS BANK
LIMITED
1896

Barclays Plaque in Hitchin Bank

He was apprenticed in London from 1819 to 1825 and trained as a chemist in Haymarket, working from 9am to 6pm six days a week.

Although his father is said not to have wanted his sons to follow him into the brewery trade, as the Quakers questioned such an occupation, William felt that he had no alternative as the family property had all been tied up in the business for more than a century. He gave up his other ambitions and joined the 'family business'.

Like his brothers, he enjoyed poetry, loved the countryside and the study of nature. He was an exceptionally well-read man.

He became very much involved in the development of Hitchin and arranged for the building of the Town hall, the Corn Exchange and a Quaker Meeting House.

In 1830 he married Eliza Clay, the daughter of William Clay of London and they had a son, William, born in 1832.

William, his father, died in Wratten, Hitchin, in 1861.

Samuel

Samuel was born on 21st August 1805 in Tilehouse Street, Hitchin. 'The Tile House' where the family lived is now numbered 25, 26 and 27.

As a child, like his brothers, he was interested in Geology and Nature Study. He was educated at Hitchin Free School before transferring to the Society of Friends School called 'Fishponds' situated near Bristol. It was here that he developed a liking for drawing and sketching.

At the age of 14 he was sent to work as an apprentice with Thomas Lindbetter, a Shipowner and Wharfinger of Southwick in Sussex. He worked on the loading of ships in Shoreham Harbour. Some time later he changed to working in Wapping Corn Market and took the opportunity to travel to Europe.

In 1826, at the age of twenty one, he was made a partner in the business of George Millward & Co. of Waterford House in Goswell Street.

He continued his drawing and painting and, in 1826, exhibited an oil painting at the Royal Academy.

In 1834 the decision was made to return to his father's brewery in Hitchin. His work there allowed him to travel extensively in the course of business. He also had time to work with his painting.

While doing this, he met John Sell Cotman and members of the Norwich School. In Norwich he met Matilda Holmes of Tivetshall, a nearby village, and they were married in the Summer of 1937.

Around this period, William frequently exhibited his pictures.

William and Matilda had three sons, Ralph, Samuel and Edwin, before Matilda died in 1849. William was devasted with his loss and immersed himself in his painting in the studio at the 'Tile House' and in the running of the brewery.

Thirteen years after the death of Matilda, he married Elizabeth Manser of Hertford.

In 1865 he suffered a stroke that incapacitated him quite considerably and on 29th March, 1870 he died in the room in which he was born.

Francis

Both William and his younger brother, Francis, born in 1816, were well-read and produced a high standard of poetry and had a passion for nature study. Francis was a man of considerable wit and charm. He trained and qualified as a barrister.

Francis married Priscilla Tindall, the daughter of William Tindall, a man of prominence in the world of shipping. In 1844, Francis and his wife made their home in 'Hatcham Manor' in Surrey, with Priscilla's father, who was instrumental in providing Francis with a great deal of work through his various contacts while he was working as a barrister. In spite of this, he forsook the bar to become a banker.

After William Tindall died, Francis sold 'Hatcham Manor' and moved to Blackheath.

After ten years of happily married life, giving Francis six children, his wife died. Francis was deeply shocked and immersed himself in his banking, writing and poetry and, of course, caring for his children.

The Lucas Family and Banking

John Dollin Bassett, Joseph Sharples and William Exton, three young men in their twenties, formed a business partnership in Leighton Buzzard in 1812. They began a banking business in a grocer's shop. They were known as Bassett, Grant & Co.

Business prospered and, in 1820, they opened a bank in Hitchin. They named this, 'The Hertfordshire Hitchin Bank'. At first the business was conducted in what were, until 1957, the Rural District Council Offices in Bancroft.

This was far from being the only banking facility in Hitchin. Savings banks and 'Friendly Societies' were formed some years before.

In the middle of 1825 there began a banking crisis throughout the country and many banks were closed. However the people of Hitchin supported their banks and the crisis was averted, the business of the banks increasing.

In 1827 Sharples and Exton severed their connection with the Leighton Buzzard bank and acquired more extensive premises at 25 High Street, Hitchin. In 1836, they took Jeffrey Lucas, a son of Joseph Lucas, the brewer, into partnership. As a result the bank became Sharples, Exton & Lucas.

For 15 years the partnership continued very successfully and the bank was firmly established in the town. When Pierson's Bank failed in 1841, Sharples, Exton and Lucas purchased the site and in a few years erected the building that now houses Barclays Bank.

The new premises were first opened for business on 7th April 1845. The building still had the same front door until March 2006. It was replaced when it became necessary to provide a ramped entrance and flooring inside for disabled customers, so avoiding the use of steps up to the till points.

Exton died in 1851 and a year later Sharples no longer took an active role in the bank. Jeffrey Lucas took his brother, Edward, and James Hack Tuke of York into partnership.

In 1855 Jeffrey Lucas died and the following year another partner, Francis Lucas, cousin of Edward and son of William, the brewer, was introduced into the business. Then the bank was known as Sharples, Tuke, Lucas & Lucas.

In 1859, Frederic Seebohm became a partner. He had married one of William Exton's daughters. His name was then added to the bank's title.

Edward Lucas entered the Bank in 1871 and, after another five years, was joined by Francis Lucas's son, William Tindall Lucas. Branches were opened in Stevenage, Hatfield and New Barnet. Further members of the Tuke and Seebohm families were added to the Board in the following years.

In 1895 James Hack Tuke retired and died a year later. In the same year Francis Lucas went to his grave.

By this time the position of private banks was threatened by the joint stock banks which had been established from 1826 and the partners found themselves in an ever-threatening situation. Together with the partners of some twenty other private banks, mostly of Quaker origin, they decided to form themselves into one joint stock company.

This new company went under the name of Barclay & Co Ltd. When the change took place, the Hitchin Bank was made one of the local Head Offices. Frederic Seebohm became a director of the new bank and William Tindall Lucas became a local director.

Since that time the Hertfordshire Hitchin Bank has been Barclays Bank and all its various branches have been absorbed into the now famous banking house.

William Tindall Lucas at 'Foxholes' in Hitchin

William, the son of Francis Lucas and Priscilla Tindall was born in Hatcham Manor, Surrey in 1848. Francis Lucas, a barrister who became a banker was living in the manor with his wife and father-in-law at this time. (see notes on Lucas Family). William was one of six children, having an older sister, Priscilla Jane, and younger brothers, Raymond and Francis Henry and younger sisters Marianna and Ann.

When William was six years old his mother died. This was a deeply felt tragedy for all of the family. Francis, perhaps, over compensated in his love and 'spoiling' of his children in their formative years.

William went to Oxford where he became an enthusiastic oarsman. He obtained a BA. Degree and from the university he went into banking, as had his father. He later developed a talent for wood carving. He and his sisters presented the elaborately carved font at St Mary's Church in Hitchin in memory of their father.

Although the members of William's family and those associated with the bank were all Quakers, from well-established families in Hitchin, William and his sister, Marianna, left the Society of Friends at an early age.

William married Frances Augusta Farmer in St Mary's Church in Hitchin on 16th April 1873. He was twenty five and she was twenty two. Frances was born in Canada. They set up their home at 'Foxholes' in Pirton Road, Hitchin and remained there for over thirty years, a house, standing in seventeen acres of land, which had been built for them.

In the first seventeen years of their marriage William and Frances produced ten children. The Census of 1881 records the family at 'Foxholes'. William, shown as a banker, and Frances, his wife aged thirty, were with their children, all born in Hitchin. They employed a cook, a parlour maid, a housemaid and a nurse, together with a Swiss nursemaid and another nursemaid, aged fifteen, from Pimlico in London.

Ten years later. William and Frances employed a French governess, as well as a cook from Cornwall, a nurse from Dorchester and five maids. They had retained none of the staff shown ten years earlier.

On the 1901 Census, William was shown as a Director of a Bank and a Justice of The Peace for Hertfordshire. Their children, Dorothy, Margaret, Cecil, Geraldine, Katherine and Everilda were still at 'Foxholes'. Archibald, Francis and Cuthbert had left home and it is probable that John, their youngest child, had died as he was not recorded as living with them. They employed a footman as well as four maids. There were no coachmen, nurses or governesses recorded as living in the house, although there were a number of other buildings close by.

It was a religious family and all of the staff were expected to attend

Morning Prayer. The family was much involved in the life of the town of Hitchin where William was a magistrate and Frances was a benefactress to St Mary's Church where she had been married. One of her daughters was the first sister in charge of the Red Cross Hospital opened in Bedford Road in 1915.

By 1901 William had built a 'Lodge' next to the house and was employing Albert Titmuss, aged fifty, as a gardener. Albert and his wife, Harriet, and their two teenage daughters lived in the 'Lodge'. Previously the family had lived in Pirton Village.

In 1910 the house and grounds were valued at £7,830.

By the end of the First World War, William Lucas had retired from Banking and a family from Norfolk came into service at the house. There was a parlour maid together with two housemaids, two kitchen maids, a butler and three gardeners. The family owned an enclosed coach, drawn by two horses, and butter was made from the milk of the Lucas family's own Jersey cows.

Foxholes was sold and William and Frances moved to Welwyn, purchasing a residence known as 'The Hall' in 1919.

They celebrated their Golden Wedding there, the event being reported in the Hertfordshire Advertiser on 21st April 1923. They remained at 'The Hall' until their deaths. William died at the age of eighty nine in June 1937 and Frances at the age of eighty seven in June 1938.

The Hall in Old Welwyn

On the north side of Church Street in Welwyn, a house was built in 1811 by John Cotton. He died in 1822 but his wife continued to live there until 1831. The house formed a part of the extensive estate of Danesbury that was bought by William Blake in 1824.

The name of the house, known previously as 'Myrtle Hall', was changed to be known as 'The Hall'.

For some years the Blake family let 'The Hall' to various people. Among them was Dr Horatio Warner in the 1860s.

Some ten years later, living in a development of the house which was erected in 1870 in the Victorian Gothic style, was James Sheppard. He was described on the 1871 census as a corn factor who was born in Plaistow in Essex in 1817. He was shown at 'The Hall', living with his daughter, Ellen Elizabeth, who was born in 1845 in Hampstead, London. With them was another daughter, Lucy Catherine, who was also born in Hampstead in 1846. James employed a cook/ housekeeper, a butler, and three maids.

In 1881, the census records James with Ellen and his younger daughter, Fiona Matilda, born in 1848 in Hampstead. He employed a cook, a butler and three maids together with a stable boy.

The 1891 census records the occupant of 'The Hall' as being Henrietta Blake, aged 78, and a widow. Henrietta was the daughter of George S. Martin and Charlotte Tucker who were married in Radford in Oxfordshire in 1811, the year that 'The Hall' was built.

Henrietta was born in Marshalswick in Hertfordshire about 1812 and she married Frederick Rudolph Blake there in 1849. Frederick was the younger brother of William John Blake and lived in Danesbury for all of his life. He was the son of William Blake and Mary and had been born on 16th April 1808 and baptised in St Mary's Church in Marylebone Road, London on 21st September of that year.

He joined the 33rd (Duke of Wellington's) Regiment as an ensign in 1825 and served for twenty seven years before becoming a Colonel in November 1852. He died at Danesbury on 23rd August, 1855 of a fever contracted at the siege of Sebastopol.

After Frederick's death, Henrietta moved to 'The Hall', as the dower house of Danesbury.

The 1891 Census showed her with a granddaughter, a grandson and a great niece. She had a housekeeper, three maids, two nurses, a butler and a groom.

She spent the last years of her life at 'The Hall' where she died in 1895. She was buried in the Blake family vault at Welwyn Church on 1st July, the last member of the family to be laid to rest there.

After her death, 'The Hall' may have been occupied by Admiral

Alexander Plantagenet Hastings, whose wife was a sister of the then owner of Danesbury, Colonel Arthur Maurice Blake. This cannot be confirmed.

About 1899, 'The Hall' was let to Francis John Riversdale Grenfell JP who lived there until the end of World War I. He served on the Church Council and his wife founded the Children's League of Pity with the object of helping poor children in London.

The Grenfells left 'The Hall' in 1919 when it was purchased by William Tindall Lucas, formerly of 'Foxholes' in Hitchin.

William T Lucas's grandson, John Kingdom Tregasse Frost, described the rambling old house, as he knew it, during the two World Wars. 'Visitors had to climb three flights of steps and stairs in order to reach the drawing room and the 'downstairs' regions were an absolute warren. The 'back-stairs' joined the main staircase immediately outside the drawing room door and each landing led to a separate colony of bedrooms. One can easily imagine the predicament and embarrassment of guests lacking a well-developed sense of direction, alone and unable to find their way to their own room.'

There were stables with stalls for four horses and a large coach house, later converted to the main garage, with a smaller garage to the left of the yard. Electric light was supplied by a high-speed paraffin engine and a heating system needed some seventy tons of solid fuel in a year.

William Lucas and his wife died shortly before World War II. Their executors decided to dispose of the house. The Rural District Council could have bought it for £1,100. but failed to see what use they could make of it, surely a regrettable decision in the light of present day prices!

At the beginning of World War II it was acquired by ICI who occupied it for some 15 years. Welwyn Hall Research Association built extensive laboratories in the grounds and sold the property in 1973.

During the following years, 'The Hall' became the subject of much discussion relating to its development, its unsafe structure, and its complete demolition. Planning applications to develop the site by destroying the listed building were refused. The building remained in a poor state of repair and nobody was prepared to pay for the necessary rebuilding and restoration.

It is believed that towards the end of the 20th Century, Rank Xerox acquired the property that was used for office accommodation for some ten years.

Still applications to demolish the supposedly unsafe building were rejected. Vandals set light to the building. It was so badly damaged by the fire that it had to be demolished. This was the second occasion when the land of two buildings of importance in Welwyn, in a conservation area, had been acquired in this way!

On the site, a new housing development took place and today, in 2010, there stands Welwyn Hall Gardens, rows of 'town houses' some eleven years old. It is a very pleasant area and well-constructed. However the construction, brought about by 'property developers' in the modern day scheme of things has meant the destruction of yet another part of Hertfordshire heritage.

The Moss Family – Hitchin, Milton Keynes

John Moss, the founder of what was to become the largest grocery business in Hitchin in the 19th century, was born in Buckingham. He was the son of John Moss, a travelling draper, and his wife, Elizabeth. He was baptised in St Mary's Church, Aylesbury in Buckinghamshire on 12th December 1816.

Elizabeth died soon after John's birth. His father married again and John was, reportedly, very unhappy in his childhood. After living in Aylesbury, his father moved to Cambridge where his daughter, John's step-sister, Maria, was born in 1827.

Young John travelled with his father in Cambridgeshire, Hertfordshire and Essex. After his father's death in Cambridge, he moved to London where he worked very hard as a grocer's porter.

In 1840, he settled in Codicote, a village outside of Stevenage, and worked from there as a travelling draper, following in his father's footsteps. A year later, he married Emma Crane who was born in that village in 1819. Their son, also named John, was born during the following year.

John and Emma moved to Stevenage at a time when the development of the railway system was starting. They lived in Middle Row where John rented a shop. It was here that their second son, William Benjamin, was born in 1844.

Every day, John served hot coffee to the navvies working on the railway from Deard's End until they reached the Wymondley cutting. He earned and learned much from his enterprise.

At this time John joined the Wesleyan Methodist Church, a decision that was to change his life and the lives of the family that followed him, for many years to come. While at Stevenage he became a Sunday School Superintendent for a period of fifteen years as well as being a chapel keeper and a Society steward.

The census of 1851 recorded the family as living in Middle Row. John was shown as a grocer and tea dealer. Apart from Emma and their two children, John's step-sister, Maria, was with them.

In 1854, the family moved to Hitchin where John worked for Mr John Smith Rose as a travelling draper. At the same time he rented a shop in Bancroft. The rent was £29 per year and his first week's takings were recorded as thirty shillings.

Whenever he was working for Mr Rose, his wife, Emma, looked after their shop which was later to become the police station in 1885. For years they had a very hard struggle to survive. Ultimately they succeeded and other shops were opened in Hitchin. 'The Old Trooper' a long-established public house, situated at the junction of Bancroft and High Street, was converted into a shop for them and this area became known as 'Moss's Corner'. Some years later, in 1900, the building was partially demolished and was reconstructed with an extra storey. The adjoining building, 13, High Street, was used by the family as storage and living accommodation before these alterations took place.

John and Emma's elder son, John, married Elizabeth who was born in Plymouth. They lived with John's parents in Hitchin where John worked as a dealer in stocks and shares. Clearly he was not interested in working in the family business but appears to have been unsuccessful in his chosen career. He did not remain in the town and moved to London where he became a journalist.

John and Elizabeth's two children, Percy and Ethel, were born in Brixton in the 1870s. The family moved to Tottenham before the children were teenagers. Here they were living in Foyle Road.

John, aged forty nine, was recorded on the census in 1891, in Gray's Inn, London, where he was shown as a journalist and sub-editor, as he had been ten years earlier. His wife and children were not with him.

While John did not 'follow in his father's footsteps' in the grocery business, his son, Percy, certainly did. Percy married Helena Ireland who was born in Dorking in Surrey. The ceremony was held in St Saviour's Church in Southwark in 1893. They had two sons and three daughters and Percy had become a journalist and a sub-editor of a London daily newspaper. At first the family lived in Gloucester Road, Tottenham before moving to Bounds Green Road in Wood Green, North London.

William Benjamin, John and Emma's younger son, began his working life as an apprentice to James Rose, for whom his father had worked. Later he moved to Kettering where he worked as an assistant in a drapery business.

He returned to Hitchin in 1868, when he married Georgina Elizabeth, the daughter of George and Mary Godfrey, who had been baptised in the Wesleyan Chapel in Luton in 1848. She was born in Pegsdon, a village outside of Hitchin. Three years later William and Georgina were recorded with their son, William Harry, aged one, when they were living in Bancroft Street.

William Benjamin became more involved in the family business and by 1869, at the age of twenty six, he was largely responsible for its management; his father, John, working in a supervisory capacity.

Throughout their lives all the members of the family were devout Wesleyan Methodists. John, became the Sunday School

Superintendent in the Chapel in Brand Street for thirty years, as well as being choirmaster, class leader and a trustee. In the course of time, William became a minister of the church and worked as a preacher for a period of sixty years.

William and Georgina had three more sons and three daughters, Ellen, Evelyn and Josephine, all born in Hitchin. Two of their sons, Hubert and Wallace, became very involved in the family business in Hitchin. Their other sons, Sydney George and William Harry were to manage branches of the business in Yorkshire.

When William Benjamin was running the business in Bancroft, his father moved to 116, Nightingale Road, Hitchin. In 1874, Kelly's Directory showed John Moss as a shopkeeper in that road, where he remained until he retired the following year.

The censuses of 1881 and 1891 show John and Emma living at 7, Bancroft. In his later life, John took up the overseership of St Ippollitts, King's Walden, Great Walden, Offley and Lilley, as well as being a tax-collector and insurance agent until 1896.

The same census recorded William, Georgina and five of their children living at 13 High Street, the property adjoining their shop. Four apprentice grocers and two servants were with them. These buildings formed 'Moss's Corner'.

The family grew as did the business, which was described at various times as 'Grocer and Tea Dealer' and as a 'Tea Dealer and Provision Merchant'. In 1895, new premises were acquired in Mill Yard.

In 1899, a branch of the business was opened at Fenny Stratford in Buckinghamshire. It was situated at 57 Aylesbury Street, between Church Street and George Street, and was only a very short distance from the old A5, Watling Street. At this time, long before the Milton Keynes By-Pass was constructed, Fenny Stratford was a thriving market town, containing several inns for the use of travellers going to and from London. Evidence of the market is shown in an old photograph of the Moss shop, where sheep pens have been placed in the road and on the paved area outside of the shop and those adjoining it. These buildings no longer exist but, certainly Moss's were trading there in

1939 before the start of World War II. Today they have been replaced by a row of more modern shops, probably built soon after the war.

One surprising fact emerges from this part of Moss's history. When the branch opened in 1899 it was described in the local directory as 'grocers and agents for W A Gilbey Ltd, wine merchants'. Certainly Gilbey's premises adjoined those of Moss and can be remembered by local residents. In view of the strict Methodists abstention from alcohol, and John Moss's claim to total abstention (see below), it does seem incongruous that they would derive part of their income from its sale. Perhaps it is no more unusual than the circumstances of the Lucas family of Quakers in Hitchin whose main source of wealth for some two hundred years came from the family brewery in the town. However, in both cases, the town benefited considerably from the wealth of the families concerned.

William Benjamin's sons, William Harry and Sydney George did not remain as part of the family business in Hitchin but moved farther away into Yorkshire.

Following his education at Kent College, Canterbury, Sydney George, went to Ripon in Yorkshire as the manager of a branch of the Hitchin firm. This was in 1899 when he was twenty three years of age. The shop stood in Queen's Street on the corner of what was called Moss's Arcade, which ran alongside the road to the bus station. Other branches of the Moss business opened in Ripon in the course of time. Sydney sat on the City Council and was Mayor of Ripon from 1929 to 1930.

The part that Methodism played in the family was illustrated by the fact that Sydney was organist and choir master of the Central Methodist Church, as well as being a Circuit Steward and Lay Preacher.

He and his wife, Mary, a Ripon girl, whom he had married in 1904, were recorded on the 1911 Census as living with their two young children, Mary, aged three, and John, aged two, at 1 Crescent Parade, a large semi-detached Victorian house on several floors a short distance from the Market Square in Ripon. Later he moved to a larger property, 'North Lodge', in North Road, only a short distance from

Crescent Parade. He died there in 1968 but the property is still owned and occupied by descendents of the Moss family.

In 1901 Sydney's brother, William, was living in 'Newall Mount' in a parish called Newall with Clifton just outside of Otley in the West Riding of Yorkshire. With him were his wife, Fanny, who was born in the area, and their two sons and a daughter. William, like Sydney was sent there to manage an extension of the grocery business which had started in Hitchin. The Moss's s shop was in the Market Place in Otley.

The 1911 Census recorded the family living at 1, Wythburn in Newall. By this time they had four more children and employed two servants.

Why the brothers went to Yorkshire in the extension of the Moss business is unknown. However both brothers were members of the Wesleyan Methodist Church as had been members of their family for many years previously. Both Ripon and Otley were towns where Methodism thrived and this may have been the reason for the choice of location. In Otley, Methodism started around 1740 and a first chapel was built there in Nelson Street in 1771. John Wesley, the founder of Methodism, preached here and visited Otley on many occasions during his journeys on horseback around the country. He developed a close friendship with the Ritchie family, who lived in Boroughgate, and stayed with them when he was in the area. The Methodist Chapel in Boroughgate was built in 1875 with a capacity for seating up to a thousand people. This was shortly before William Moss arrived in the area and when Methodism was growing rapidly.

By the beginning of the 20th Century, the business of W.B Moss & Sons had over thirty employees and members of the family had moved to large properties in Bedford Road, Hitchin.

John Moss, aged eighty five and a widower by this time, was living at No 6 where he had a housekeeper. His wife, Emma, died five years before him and he died a sudden but peaceful death on 25th March 1903, aged eighty six. He attributed his cheerfulness and exuberant spirit to being a teetotaller for all of his life!

William Benjamin, 57, and Georgina, together with son, Wallace, and two daughters, were living at No 1. Their son, Hubert, aged twenty eight, and his wife, Gertrude, then twenty three, as well as a newly-born son, William Donald, were at No 2. Neither of these properties was owned by the Moss family which, at this time, were valued at £1134 and £730 respectively.

The 1911 Census recorded William still at No 1 Bedford Road with his wife and son, Wallace, and a servant. Hubert, his son, was living at 6 Bancroft. He and his wife, Gertrude, had no more children by this time. William Donald, aged eleven, was at school.

Seven years later Moss's had become the largest provision merchant ever known in the area. In addition to dealing with tea and groceries, the firm also became china, glass and furniture dealers with warehouses and a bacon curing factory in Portmill Lane.

William B Moss bought 'The Croft', a beautiful house in Bancroft, from James Hack Tuke, the banker who became a partner in the Hitchin Bank in 1851. The house had been built in the early 15th Century and had wonderful gardens at the rear. It was renovated and embellished in the 17th and 19th Centuries and contained a library, oak panelled rooms, and fireplaces made with traditional blue and white Dutch tiles. James Tuke restructured the house in a Gothic style and decorated the walls with ornamental tiles.

When William moved there, he used the house next door, No 10, as a furniture showroom. On his death, his son, Hubert, and his family occupied the property. The house was virtually destroyed in 1964 to make way for modern 'shopping development'.

William died in 1927. He was a great lover of horses and a keen huntsman. When he could no longer ride to hunt meetings, he still attended, driving by car and receiving a great welcome on arrival. Apart from his considerable involvement with the Methodist Church, he also served for nine years as a councillor on Hitchin Urban District Council.

In the early 1930s, Hubert purchased 'Foxholes' in Pirton Road, the home of the Lucas family. However he never actually moved into the property and, in 1937, was still living at 11 Bancroft. Wallace Moss, Hubert's brother, was living at 24 Bedford Road at this time.

The family purchased a number of other properties in Hitchin including the building which was later to become the Museum, Art Gallery and Library. This house, named 'Agadir', was built in 1825 and was owned by George Kershaw, the proprietor of the Swan Inn. It doubled in size over the years and its name was changed to 'Charnwood House'. The Moss brothers, Hubert and Wallace, acquired this building which stood in Paynes Park and generously gave it to the town in 1936. It underwent many alterations before it was used as a library in September 1938. An extension, built in 1965, was occupied by the library and, as a result, both the library and the museum were able to expand.

Hubert also bought 'Elmside' in Bedford Road, the home of Lawson Thompson and his sisters, Mary and Margaret. He left this house and garden to be used by the Methodist Church as a hall and a home for the elderly.

No 1 Bedford Road, the former home of William Benjamin Moss, is used as a home for the elderly at the present time.

The Devitts in Northaw

'Northaw Place' had been leased for use as a preparatory school until 1928. At this time the 'school' moved to Dering in Kent and Frederic Hall transferred the ownership of 'Northaw Place' to his children before making his will at this time. The Hall sisters sold the property to Philip Devitt in 1929. Renovations and alterations on the house began. It took the best part of a year to convert the school into a private house and it was not until 1930 that the Devitt family was able to move into the residence where they were certainly no strangers.

Throughout the time that the Devitt family lived in 'Foxholes' and in the following years at 'Northaw Place', Philip devoted his working life to the nautical college at Pangbourne. All prospective cadets were interviewed by him in the London office before they could start any course at the college. His work load increased dramatically as his father became ill before his death in 1923. Philip travelled to the college at least once every week, accompanied on most occasions by his wife.

He was honoured to receive a visit from The Prince of Wales, later the Duke of Windsor, on Founders Day in 1927. For this occasion, Philip bought a Rolls Royce and his chauffeur drove all of the Devitt family from Hitchin to Pangbourne where they stayed in an hotel overnight before the royal visit and prize-giving on the next day.

Soon after the Devitt family returned to 'Northaw Place', developments took place at Pangbourne. In 1931, there was a change in the constitution of the college. A Board of Governors was set up and Philip was the first Chairman. A new company was formed, The Devitt & Moore Nautical College Ltd.

Philip was created a Baronet, Sir Philip Henry Devitt of Pangbourne, on 25th June 1931 and he became a Justice of the Peace in Hertfordshire.

This was certainly a notable year, for on 7th August, Dorothy gave birth to twins. Prior to the twins' birth, Dorothy had left Northaw to stay with her sister-in-law, Helen, who lived in 6 Hanover Terrace, Regents Park. The move was made so that she could be near her London doctors as well as receiving her sister-in-law's support. She was forty four at this time and Philip was fifty five. The twins were born in Hanover Terrace. Sadly one of them was born with what is now known as Downs Syndrome and so two of the five daughters of Philip and Dorothy were seriously disabled. Dorothy Susan, later known as Sue, and Bridget Helen, known as Biddy, were baptised in Northaw Church on 3rd October by the Bishop Buckingham when Margaret and Elsie, two of Dorothy's sisters were godparents.

As well as being Chairman of the Governors and a Founder of the Devitt and Moore Nautical College in Pangbourne and sole partner in the firm of Devitt and Moore of 84 Leadenhall Street EC3., Philip was Deputy Chairman of the Royal Alfred Aged Merchant Seamen's Institution, a Vice-President of the Marine Society, Vice-Chairman of the Board of Sailors' Home, in Dock Street, East London, Chairman of Annual National Service for Seafarers and Hon. Member of Hon. Company of Master Mariners.

He also became a Governor of his old school, the Loretto School in Edinburgh.

Pangbourne College developed satisfactorily during the next seven years but, at the outbreak of World War Two, problems abounded, particularly in terms of staffing. The Captain Superintendent who had been at the college for the past four years was recalled to the Navy, as were other members of the staff, and the possibility of finding replacements was not encouraging, as was the case in many similar institutions. Philip Devitt made the decision to take on the work of the superintendent himself.

He closed the London office of Devitt & Moore, and, with Dorothy and their five daughters, left 'Northaw Place', leasing the property to Middlesex County Council, when it was then used as a Children's Home.

In later years plans were drawn up to convert 'Northaw Place', a listed building, into four homes, together with five houses in the grounds, adjoining the house. The old house is still in need of considerable repair at the present time. In spite of the intentions of 1987, little has been achieved in the preservation of the building itself.

Philip and his family moved into 'Devitt House' in Pangbourne where they faced many difficulties during the war. Philip had numerous problems to solve in maintaining the education of his pupils and assuring that the college survived until staff returned. Few changes were made during the war years but one notable occasion provided a lasting memory. King George VI and Princess Elizabeth visited the college on Founders Day in 1943 and the occasion was a great success. It was a tribute to the contribution that Old Pangbournians had made. Sadly many had died during their active service.

The college returned to normal after the war and Sir Philip, who had celebrated his 70th birthday in 1946, left 'Devitt House' with his family and moved to Englefield Green, a short distance away. His health deteriorated rapidly and he died suddenly on 5th June 1947. Without his determination to ensure the development and the survival of the college, a cause to which he devoted his whole life, there is no doubt that Pangbourne would not have become the successful school that it is today.

As Philip had no male heir the Baronetcy became extinct.

Philip's brother Howson, who had been a governor of Pangbourne since 1938, was not prepared to devote the time to being Chairman of the Nautical College and took over the role on a temporary basis until Philip's nephew, Sir Thomas Gordon Devitt, was persuaded to carry on the Devitt tradition in 1948. He remained as Chairman until 1961 when he retired through ill-health. Seven years later, the status of Pangbourne changed once more. The Nautical College became Pangbourne College and is now an educational establishment for both boys and girls but the traditions and the ethos of the school retain much of the Devitt creation.

9

Some Conclusions

Perhaps the generosity of the Kidston family in funding the rebuilding of Northaw Parish Church in 1881, together with the provision of a vicarage and other additions, illustrates the belief of some people of their responsibility towards the 'church' and society in general. There may have been a number of other reasons but we shall never know the answer.

Several other families have provided similar examples. Enosh Durant paid for the construction of St Peter's Church in Arkley in 1840, as well as an Infant School there and two others close by. John Trotter paid for the building of Christ Church, Barnet as well as a school building and almshouses in Ridge. Robert Bevan paid for the construction of Christ Church, Cockfosters and the adjoining Trent School and Henry Toulmin provided St Mary's Church for his tenants at Childwick Green, as well as a schoolroom to educate adults. Sir John Maple enlarged this in his time there.

The strength of 'the church' is evident in the attitude of the wealthy towards education. Frequently sons who were sent to university, completed courses and took degrees in religious studies, qualifying as prospective clergymen. Undoubtedly there is considerable evidence of clergymen marrying to enhance their financial status or to increase their prospects in their chosen profession.

The effect of religious beliefs in business is readily apparent. The Quaker families in Hitchin worked together, in various commercial enterprises, particularly in banking, and gained considerable benefits from within their group. At the same time the Moss family who were staunch Wesleyan Methodists prospered in the same town.

The 'landed gentry', who built their country seats in Northaw and many similar areas, provided employment for those less affluent. The population of Northaw Village increased dramatically when the families of those working in the large houses maintained their own families in the cottages of the village. Others settled in the village to provide services for the gentry.

Gradually as the larger houses became derelict or destroyed, were converted into flats, offices or were left unoccupied, so their occupants left the village. There are surely few people living in Northaw today who are socially deprived in any way. Cottages have given way to new and extended houses or other radical conversions.

There are no shops, no post office, not even one based in one of the two remaining public houses, which trade in the village. The Sun and "The Two Brewers" remain, of course, because the motor car enables people to come into Northaw and enjoy what still appears to be its village status. Those living in Northaw can travel to all the shops and supermarkets in neighbouring areas in a matter of minutes. The village store is a thing of the past.

What of Northaw Church which still stands in all its glory, the centre piece of the village? Today a member of the clergy is shared with the ever-increasing community of Cuffley. No longer do the families of the gentry, living in their large houses, walk to the church with all of their families as a matter of routine, particularly on a Sunday morning. No longer do the villagers sit at the back of the church or doff their hats as the wealthy pass by them outside, neither in Northaw nor in Ridge, where the Trotters worshipped with the Ebbs family who would offer them the same respect.

What happened to the 'landed gentry'? As has been seen, many of the young men, who were likely to have ensured the continuation of these families, were killed in either of the two World Wars. The Hall family lost both sons and the continuation of the family name.

The emphasis changed from families having a country seat, as well as a place in the town or city where they worked, to having a 'holiday home' or 'seat' abroad. As is evident in the research, many of the families lived and worked in the Caribbean countries, in South America or in India, a practice which was to grow with the modernisation of shipping and with the development of air travel.

A number of the families researched in this work did not inherit their wealth initially. It was through their hard work and the initiative of their ancestors that they became accepted in 'society'. This was certainly true of the Durant, Joel, Greene and Moss families who all became wealthy enough to be accepted by the gentry. The Singer family experienced the difficulties of breaking into their local 'society' in Paignton.

One great leveller in social standing appears to have been, and still is, an interest and success in horse riding, hunting and horse-racing. An example of this is clearly seen in the Joel family whose success in the field of horse racing led them to socialise with royalty in this 'Sport of Kings'. However it must be remembered that they were fabulously rich diamond merchants as well!

Philip Devitt, who was passionate about horse racing, and who would never willingly miss any of the 'Classics', spent time socialising with those involved in this 'sport'. Undoubtedly he would have shown a keen interest in the Northaw Stud, as would his family who from early days had been taught to ride in their estates and in and around the village. Whereas there would have been much involvement in the local Hunt at this time, today hunting, as such, has been banned and it is seldom that one sees horse riders in the village. However, there is one annual 'point to point' race meeting held in the fields of Northaw!

The days of the 'London Season' and 'coming-out balls' for 'debutantes' have long since disappeared. London's society has become cosmopolitan. Many of the richest people are involved in the entertainment industry, commerce and industry and do not look to their families for wealth and the enhancement of their careers.

Whereas flats or apartments in London are still commonplace, country estates are not. Many have either fallen into disrepair, have been converted into flats or offices, are unoccupied or have been taken over by The National Trust.

As long as the Church of St Thomas à Becket stands, so the treasured memories of Northaw and all that it has stood for during the past centuries will be recalled and will remain. Here one can find, buried side by side, the Halls, Polands and Priestleys of 'Northaw Place', the Le Blanc family of 'Northaw House', the Kidstons of 'Nyn Manor' and the Roddicks of 'The Hook'.

Many of the buildings, and most of the people, of Northaw of days gone by are no more but they have left the records of some really interesting and often inspirational events. They and we are nothing but the memories that we create.

10

Sources of Information

I acknowledge reference to the following sources of the information used in this work.

Hertfordshire, Devon, Suffolk Record Offices, Libraries & Archives & Metropolitan Archives

	Parish Registers, Censuses from 1841 to 1911 in England
Hertfordshire Archives	1910 Inland Revenue Survey
Library	Kelly's Directories = Commercial and Private Hertfordshire Directories
	'Hertfordshire Countryside' Volume XXIX

'Welwyn & Hatfield Times' October 1995

Society of Genealogists	Birth, Marriage & Death records
	County Records
	School and University records
	Burke's Peerage
	Crockford's

Hertfordshire Libraries	Oxford Dictionary of National Biography (OU Press)
Reference Department	Torquay Central Library

Information has been gained from a number of Internet sources, in particular Wikipedia.

<u>Reference Books</u>

Page

3	Cuffley and Northaw Past	Millington & Higgs	Broxbourne Press
5b	Stanley Kubrick – The Complete Films	Paul Duncan	Taschen
	Christiane Kubrick	Marina Vaizey	Warner Books
9	Wisbech	Robert Bell	Francis Frith
10	Paignton & South Devon		Ward Lock

	Torquay & South Devon		Ward Lock
	Paignton	John Pike	Torbay B C
	Paignton Parish Church	Arthur R Day	Newton Printers
11	St Albans Cathedral		Jarrold Publications
12	Ashburton	Frances Pilkington	Devon Books
	Ashburton of Yesteryear	John Germon and Pete Webb	Obelisk Publications
	Torbay	John Whitton	Bossiney Books
16	The Trelawnys	Carol Vivian	
17	Villages of South Hamms	John Legge	Obelisk Publications
20	'Spacious Days'	Nesta Webster	
	History of The Bevan Family	Audrey Gamble	Heardley Bros.
21	'As It Happened'	Rt.Hon C Attlee	Bodley Head
21	'A Spastic in the Family'	Theordora Devitt	
24	Greene King	Richard Wilson	Bodley Head
	Brewers in Hertfordshire	Dr Alan Whittaker	University of Hertfordshire
28	A History of Berkhamsted School	B H Garnons Williams	Hazell, Watson & Viney Ltd
28	'A Sort of Life'	Graham Greene	Bodley Head
	'The Other Man'	Marie Allain	Bodley Head
	A Life in Letters	Graham Greene	Abacus
	Bygone Berkhamsted	Percy Britchnell	White Crescent Press
30	Pangbourne College	L C Stephens	Dovecote Press
34	A Quaker Journal (Vol.1 & 2)	William Lucas	Hutchinson & Co
31	Old Hitchin	Alan Fleck and Helen Poole	Phillimore
35	Barclays Bank Ltd	Tuke & Gillman	Barclays Bank
36	Memories of Welwyn	Gordon Longmead	New Concept Publishing

Other General Reference Material:

Brewer's Britain & Ireland	Ayto & Crofton	Weindenfield & Nicholson
The Hertfordshire, Suffolk & Cambridgeshire Village Books	Fed. of Women's Institutes	Countryside Books

I offer my sincere thanks to:

The staff of Hertfordshire Libraries and Archives, of Enfield Archives and Hitchin Museum and Library

The National Horseracing Museum – Newmarket

The Bursar of Berkhamsted School

Mr L C Stephens of Pangbourne College

The Matron of 'Foxholes' in Hitchin

Mr and Mrs Kelsall of St Alban's Cathedral

Mr Bob Hutchinson, Mr Peter Nicholson and the Vicar of St Andrew's Church in Hamble-le-Rice

Mr Carl Pender of Southampton

Most of all I would offer my love and thanks to my dear family and friends who have helped me so much in writing this book. I offer it to them as a token of my gratitude.

Peter D West

11
Family Connections

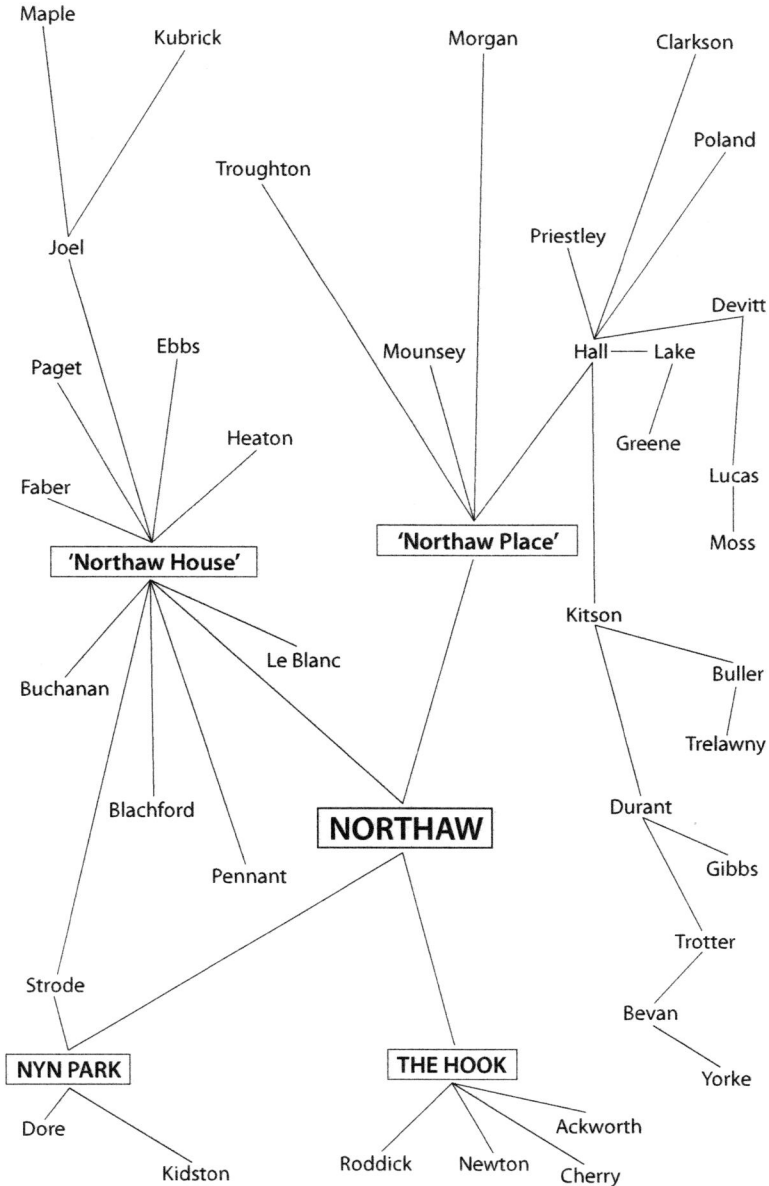

Maple

Kubrick

Morgan

Clarkson

Poland

Troughton

Priestley

Devitt

Joel

Ebbs

Mounsey

Hall —— Lake

Paget

Heaton

Greene

Lucas

Faber

Moss

'Northaw House'

'Northaw Place'

Buchanan

Le Blanc

Kitson

Buller

Trelawny

Blachford

Durant

NORTHAW

Gibbs

Pennant

Trotter

Strode

Bevan

NYN PARK

THE HOOK

Yorke

Dore

Ackworth

Kidston

Roddick   Newton

Cherry

12

Family Trees

The Devitt Family

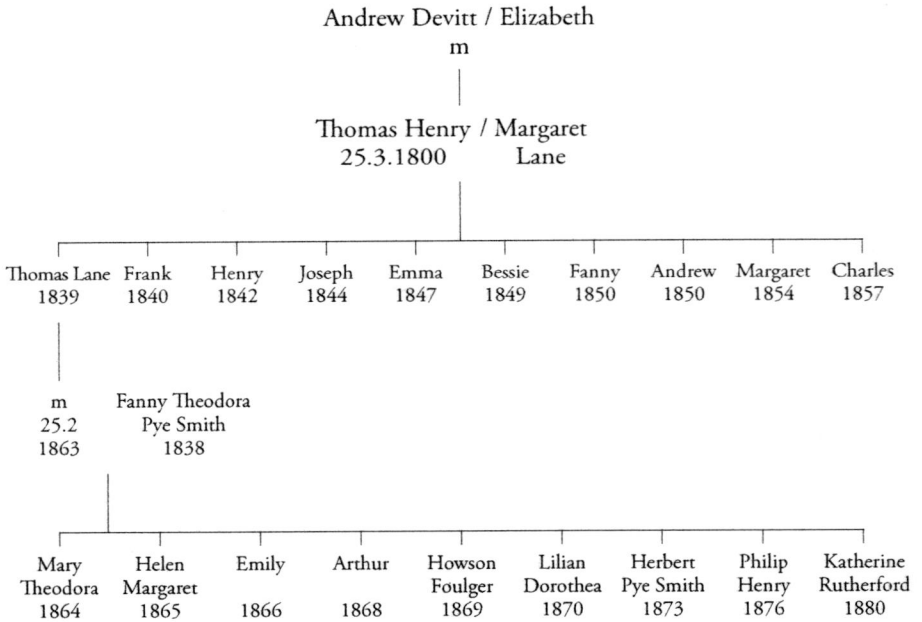

Andrew Devitt / Elizabeth
m

Thomas Henry / Margaret
25.3.1800   Lane

Thomas Lane	Frank	Henry	Joseph	Emma	Bessie	Fanny	Andrew	Margaret	Charles
1839	1840	1842	1844	1847	1849	1850	1850	1854	1857

m   Fanny Theodora
25.2   Pye Smith
1863   1838

Mary Theodora	Helen Margaret	Emily	Arthur	Howson Foulger	Lilian Dorothea	Herbert Pye Smith	Philip Henry	Katherine Rutherford
1864	1865	1866	1868	1869	1870	1873	1876	1880

The Hall Family

Some of the Children and Grandchildren of Thomas and Mary Hall

Thomas Hall / Mary Appleton Grainger
1767-1851   1781

m
1802
Yorkshire

Thomas Grainger Hall / Eliza Kitson   Henry Hall / Elizabeth Stevens
1803-1881   1808-1899   1819-1896   1813-1875

m   m
1831   1849
Devon   Cambridge

Thomas Lane   Frank   Henry   Mary Ann   Margaret   Charles
1839   1840   1842   1856   1854   1857

The Greene Family

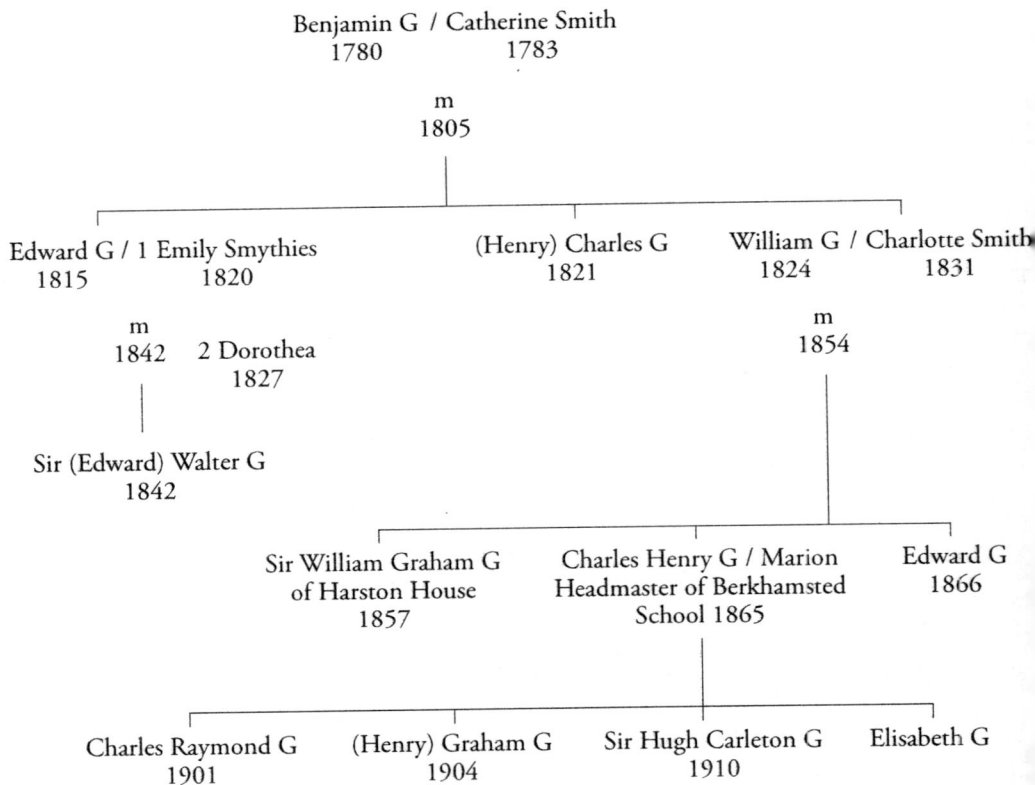

Benjamin G / Catherine Smith
1780   1783

m
1805

Edward G / 1 Emily Smythies
1815   1820

(Henry) Charles G
1821

William G / Charlotte Smith
1824   1831

m
1842   2 Dorothea
1827

m
1854

Sir (Edward) Walter G
1842

Sir William Graham G
of Harston House
1857

Charles Henry G / Marion
Headmaster of Berkhamsted
School 1865

Edward G
1866

Charles Raymond G
1901

(Henry) Graham G
1904

Sir Hugh Carleton G
1910

Elisabeth G

The Kitson Family

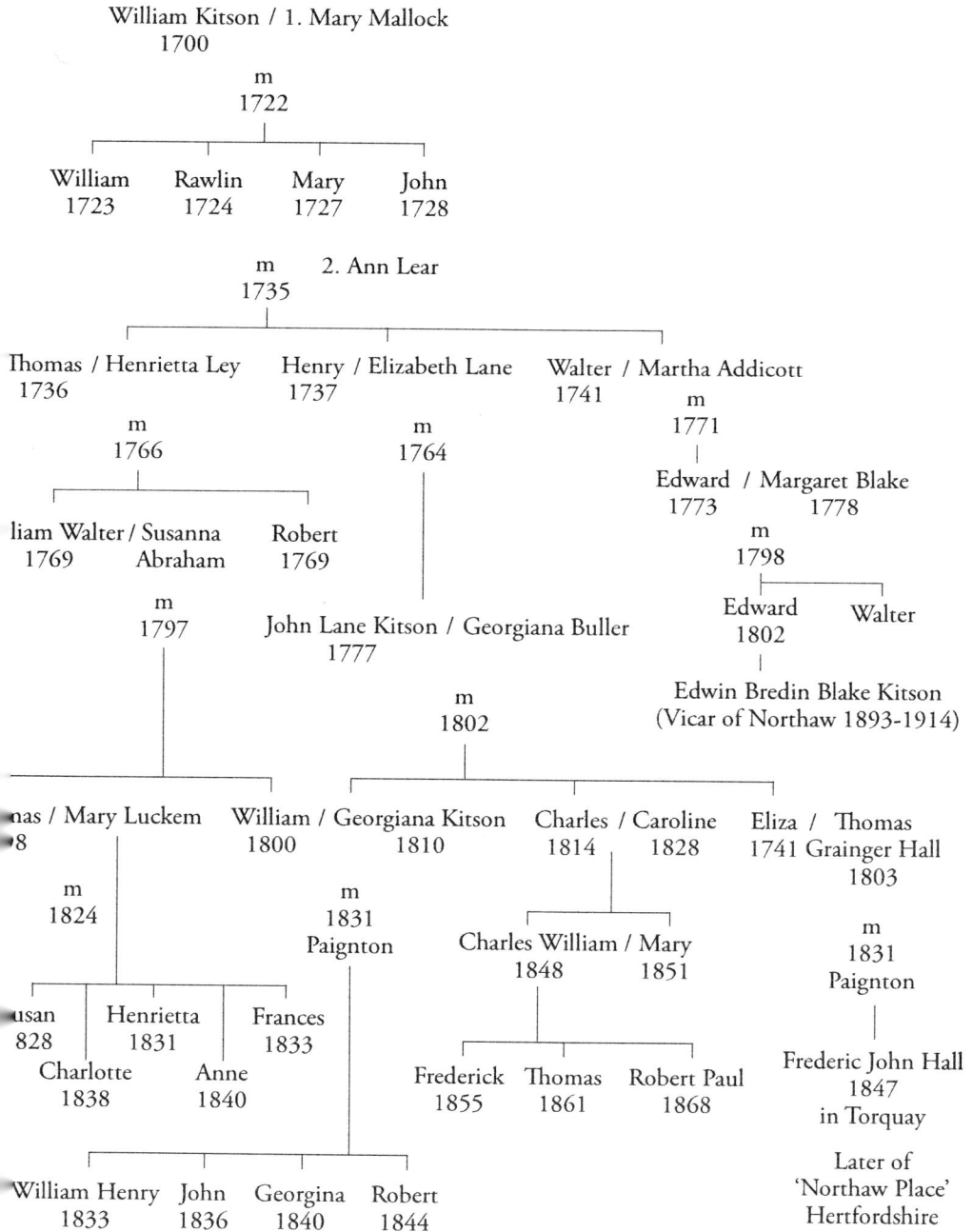

William Kitson / 1. Mary Mallock
1700

m
1722

William	Rawlin	Mary	John
1723	1724	1727	1728

m   2. Ann Lear
1735

Thomas / Henrietta Ley   Henry / Elizabeth Lane   Walter / Martha Addicott
1736   1737   1741

m   m   m
1766   1764   1771

Edward / Margaret Blake
1773   1778

m
1798

liam Walter / Susanna   Robert
1769   Abraham   1769

Edward   Walter
1802

m
1797

John Lane Kitson / Georgiana Buller
1777

Edwin Bredin Blake Kitson
(Vicar of Northaw 1893-1914)

m
1802

nas / Mary Luckem   William / Georgiana Kitson   Charles / Caroline   Eliza / Thomas
8   1800   1810   1814   1828   1741 Grainger Hall
                                                                                          1803

m   m   Charles William / Mary   m
1824   1831   1848   1851   1831
                         Paignton   Paignton

usan   Henrietta   Frances   Frederick   Thomas   Robert Paul   Frederic John Hall
828   1831   1833   1855   1861   1868   1847
Charlotte   Anne   in Torquay
1838   1840

William Henry   John   Georgina   Robert   Later of
1833   1836   1840   1844   'Northaw Place'
                                                                                     Hertfordshire